FINDING FIFTY

FINDING FIFTY

A MEMOIR OF RISING IN MIDLIFE

JILL CARLYLE

Published by The Empowered Press

https://www.theempoweredpress.com

Cover design by: Onur Aksoy

Photography by: Yildimir Danisman

ISBN: 978-1-957430-01-0 (paperback)

ISBN: 978-1-957430-02-7 (Kindle)

ISBN: 978-1-1957430-03-4 (PDF)

For Steve.
Thank you for allowing me to cry, to evolve, to survive.
Happy Fourth, baby.
I love you.

Sometimes all we have are our stories. This is mine.

—JC

AUTHOR'S NOTE

This is a work of nonfiction. The stories I share in this book directly result from my personal experiences. To protect the cast of characters, most names and identifying characteristics have been changed. This is a memoir, and I am its narrator. These are the memories of my life, conversations, and how I remember them.

FOREWORD

~

In every hero's journey, the hero does everything in their power to overcome obstacles, so they can then transform their own life - and perhaps the lives of some of the people living in their immediate circle. This is what Jill Carlyle has done in the first fifty years of her life. She has taken on the daunting task of changing the trajectory of her life and has done this by reviving and healing the younger parts of herself who were still suffering, still upending her current adult days. In this powerful memoir, she has reconnected with them and courageously restored their living voice.

She tells of "the seven-year-old who learned her brother didn't want her around, the twelve-year-old whose mother told her it would have been easier to accept a diagnosis of cancer than pregnancy, the thirteen-year-old whose father made her smoke an entire pack of cigarettes for experimenting with them, the pregnant sixteen-year-old who was forced to have an abortion, the woman with multiple marriages, the high school dropout who later became a college graduate and professor. Every age and every experience shaped the person I am."

In *Finding Fifty: A Memoir of Rising in Midlife*, Jill shares her very personal story about the gut-wrenching challenges she has navigated in her quest for the intangibles we all covet - being seen, loved, and fully accepted for who we are - in our essence.

She writes with a style that is clear, deliberate, and rich in detail, taking the reader from the recounting of the traumas she endured as a child, to the methods she later found that reset her thinking and continue to repair old mistaken beliefs about herself.

As I read her manuscript, I involuntarily winced more than once from my own empathic response to her wounding – a nod to her unwavering ability to pen her truth. These are not easy words for anyone to write. But there is hope in Jill's words. Her description of traumatic moments is balanced with stories of the quiet and evocative triumphs she still celebrates today. In a breakthrough moment, Jill shares the first time she heard her own soul, "I stopped running, kicking, screaming, flailing. I sat in the stillness and listened to my soul. I'd never heard her speak. The voice was mine, I recognized her in an instant. She sounded whole. She'd been in there for far too long."

I am familiar with the very human experience of living through trauma and wanting the pain to stop. Of the seven billion people in this world, I believe all of us know trauma. In my own professional life, I assist people to locate the suffering younger parts of themselves who are still, as Jill says, "in there," and bring them safely home, into present time. This inner work revises and updates the *false* life story perpetrated on us by people who themselves suffered. Once we clear the old emotional holding from our psyche, we can see the deeper story of who I believe we truly are; beautiful spirits here to experience a human life, offering moments of both joy and challenge.

Within the pages of this gritty, hopeful, and ultimately

uplifting memoir, this is what Jill Carlyle has accomplished. She has written one woman's account of how to stay the course during the challenges, and as the fog clears, to follow what lights the spirit and frees the soul.

Shuna Morelli
    Founder BodyMind Bridge Institute
    www.shunamorelli.com

Shuna Morelli, MS LMT CH is the founder and director of The BodyMind Bridge Institute in Steilacoom, Washington. She has developed the BodyMind Bridge Method of Self-Healing, a breakthrough whole-mind system that unites conscious awareness of the deep creative levels of our mind with the innate wisdom of the physical body.

INTRODUCTION

I have come to believe over and over again that what is most important to me must be spoken, made verbal, and shared, even at the risk of having it bruised or misunderstood.
~Audre Lorde

On August 26, 2019, I found fifty, although the lead-in to the big 5-0 was not for the faint of heart. After nearly a lifetime of swimming, what seemed like upstream, I decided on my forty-ninth birthday to write my story—I found courage.

The bridge between forty-nine and fifty produced an onslaught of emotions: feelings of insecurity, the sadness of loss, the humility to apologize to those I've hurt, but most importantly, the acceptance of self—the ability to tell my story without guilt or shame. As I sit, pencil in hand (I'm old school), recording thoughts in my favorite "Ideas" journal, I suddenly remember turning twenty and thinking how old fifty sounded and the seemingly infinite years ahead before reaching that milestone. Hell, at the time, I doubted I would even live long enough to see fifty because, at twenty, I knew everything (didn't you?). At twenty, I didn't realize that life would shift in as many directions as it did. I also didn't understand how the first twenty years of my life would shape the next thirty. I hadn't the slightest idea that I would forever carry the memories of my seven-year-old self or the lasting effects of a lifetime of emotional abandonment. I didn't grapple with any of this until I began writing my story.

Fifty is a game-changer, a life-altering, death-defying, self-defining time in a woman's life. And for the icing on the cake, there's menopause. My twenty-year-old self couldn't even pronounce the word, and now I'm living it. It's hit me harder than anything I've experienced physically and emotionally.

I follow some of the bravest women on the planet (virtually, of course), who share their voices, wisdom, courage, and empathy for the human race. Women like Glennon Doyle, Elizabeth Gilbert, Sandra Cisneros, Audre Lorde, and Brené Brown (you'll see some of these SHEros quoted in the book) whose fearlessness encourages me to speak my truth. These women have no idea who I am, but they are my cheerleaders and inspiration for writing *Finding Fifty*; I discovered how freeing it is to reflect on my life even when the reflection in the figurative mirror isn't easy to admire. I learned the deeper I dig, the more liberated I become. And through it all, I have found freedom from a past I cannot control and a future that I deserve.

Dr. Brené Brown writes in *Braving the Wilderness*:

> In these uncertain and risky moments of vulnerability, I search for inspiration from the brave innovators and disruptors whose courage feels contagious [...] I do this so that when I need them, when I'm living in my fear [...] most important while watching over my shoulder, they put up with very little of my bullshit.

In one of her "Coffee and Revolution" episodes, *New York Times* bestselling author Glennon Doyle told me to "write like someone who's never heard of shame; write like someone who's been forgiven for being human." So, here I am.

There's a bit of my story in all of us—not the same story—but the shared space of self-deprecating thoughts, feelings of failure, and the dread of judgment. Those thoughts keep us from living our best life. Writing *Finding Fifty* helped me shed those layers and dig deep into the very root of my person. I will revisit *Finding Fifty*, often adding to the story of my life. I'd love to hear from you and perhaps weave our stories together. Who knows what finding sixty, seventy, or eighty will look like?

Listen, I'm not here to pretend things are perfect; this isn't a Facebook post. *Finding Fifty* is about real life. Starting over, starting fresh: reflecting, resetting, and reinventing.

What I hope to do, in between the front and back matter of this memoir, is to share my battles and victories but also, more importantly, *connect.*

I invite you to keep reading. I think you will find that we are more alike than different. Hold my hand; I promise to hold your heart. Let's find fifty together.

PROLOGUE

*A*t 43 years old, college had always been a dream of mine. But for most of my life, that dream seemed far beyond my reach. Since the year I quit high school, I lived with shame: the shame of not finishing high school, the shame of not going to college, the shame of not conforming to what others thought I should be according to their socially constructed timeline. So, I lived in the trenches of self-deprecation, believing I wasn't good enough. The feeling of shame bore embarrassment, and out of embarrassment spun a web of lies to follow. Nearly 30 years of lying about who I was—hell, even now, standing in my truth, seeing it in black and white scares the shit out of me—I'm bringing my brave, but believing in myself has always been a tall order.

For most of my adult life, my mother pleaded with me to get my GED, but I was paralyzed with the fear of failure. Even though she and my father signed the papers allowing me to drop out of high school, she kept at me to get my high school equivalency diploma. And it wasn't that I was rebelling against her, quite the opposite. I didn't believe in *myself*. My self-esteem was never any better than the lies I allowed to swirl in my head, taking up valuable space, reminding me I wasn't smart enough to pass a high school equivalency exam.

You're a high school dropout. An embarrassment to your family. Unlovable. I subconsciously kept repeating what I'd heard about myself for most of my life. The lies I was told as a child became the truths of my adulthood. I was the product of dysfunctional conditioning. I was broken, beat down, and emotionally defeated —a direct result of my childhood. My mind played tricks on me for years, and the enemy was constantly breaking my spirit. I was a prisoner of my shame and secrets.

Very few people knew that I dropped out of school. It was the postmark of a past I tried to escape. I lived inside that lie for many years, never disclosing to anyone that I was a "quitter," as my father would say. I'd hear the whisper of my mother's words, "you don't look like a high school dropout, Jill. No one needs to know, and they will never guess as long as you keep up your looks and stay quiet."

What does a high school dropout look like? I asked myself for years. My mother's words encouraged me to bury the truth inside a lifetime of lies. That is how I navigated throughout my adulthood: one lie after another, but at 43, I took action: I wanted a college degree, and I was going to get one. I reset my life, and although I had my sights set on reaching that milestone, I still had to get to the starting line; that meant getting my GED. I created a plan for myself. I told no one what I was doing; I didn't want any distractions or naysayers giving me their ten-cent opinions. And I didn't want to explain myself to those who already believed I graduated from high school. Above all, it petrified me to disclose my shameful secret to Steve, my new boyfriend. We'd been dating for about six months, and life was as close to perfect as it had ever been. I wasn't ready to own the truth out of fear of abandonment from the life of happiness that I finally created. I was a single mom and a professional working musician playing gigs five to six nights a week and dating my now-husband since the beginning of the year.

The timing worked out well for me. I could keep up the facade; no one would be the wiser to my studying and then sitting for the exam —my daughter would be in school, and I would spend most of the day studying. During the week, Steve was 160 miles away on the other coast of Florida. My secret was safe.

After weeks of preparation, I finally felt ready to tackle the beast that had been taunting me since I was sixteen. I paid the fees and scheduled the test. My anxiety was at an all-time high. I was nervous, specifically about the math portion (my weakest subject). At my core, I was fighting against myself. One side told the other I wasn't good enough, smart enough, or strong enough. My sabotaging self worked ferociously to oppress and tell me I was merely an imposter of a decent human being. I didn't deserve the same choices and opportunities that "good people" were afforded. I never considered myself a "good person." The other side of my soul was fervently trying to scrub the negative labels of my childhood, my person, off my stained past. This internal battle was on rewind as I walked into the testing room, sat down, and waited for the instructions.

I didn't expect to see as many people taking the GED. I had this vision of only me, in the room, alone, or maybe seated with just a few other "losers" like myself. It reminded me of the label my father had given women who were, for whatever reason, forced to accept state aid to help with medical care or put food on the table for their families. They weren't all black or Latino or poorly dressed. They didn't have missing teeth, ripped or dirty clothes, and they didn't smell. There was no stereotype. Everyone there was human, not a socially constructed ideology. Diverse people, from all cultures, sitting in the same room together, taking the same test, reaching their personal best, showing up for themselves. It felt like what community should feel like: without judgment, questions, or explanations, just a common goal in the space of encouragement, everyone welcomed and accepted. I didn't know these people, yet I felt a camaraderie with them. I wanted to hug them all and scream, "Look what we're doing!"

I could be myself in that room, with those people. I didn't have to be afraid that they wouldn't accept me or say, "Sorry. You don't have your high school diploma. Get the fuck out. You aren't welcome here. You don't qualify to be here."

Nope. They gave me a seat, "Come in and sit down; you belong here. Take your test, be yourself; we're here to cheer you on." That's what their actions told me.

The test proctor finished with the instructions. Row by row, we walked to the front of the auditorium-style room, picked up a pencil, test booklet, and Scantron. I was in the front row, and I met everyone's gaze with intent and pride and smiled as they walked back to their seats. All races, genders, and ages (sixteen and over) had a purpose that day. It was one of the first times I felt I had control over my decisions and freedom over my truth.

The test was lengthy, an all-day affair. The math portion was first, and I was happy to get that out of the way. My heart was beating so loud I could hear the echo in my brain. Cold beads of sweat collected on my forehead.

Why the hell does there have to be math?

But, once I started, I was glad to get my weakest subject out of the way. Science followed, then social studies, and finally my strongest subject, language arts and writing. The test couldn't have been presented in more perfect order. Although my brain was fatigued, my strongest subject carried me to the finish line.

After eight hours, two breaks, and four sections, I finished the test. After 28 years of looking for and finally finding the courage to do it, I completed the whole damn thing. I could almost hear my mom's feet jumping up and down from the ceiling of heaven. My mother and I struggled with a strained relationship for the better part of my life, but the desire to make her proud never subsided. I put the pencil down and closed my test booklet. I looked around to see who remained, hanging in for the long haul. The room was about half full. I didn't know everyone's story, but I'd just closed the first half of mine.

I slid out of the desk, stretched my stiff legs and back, grabbed my belongings, test paraphernalia, and handed it over to the proctor.

"Thank you, Ms..." looking through her bifocals resting on the tip of her nose; she found my name on the front of the Scantron, "...Ms. Wilson. Is this your correct address?" Her voice was barely a whisper to not disrupt the rest of the test takers.

"Yes." I smiled and looked her in the eyes.

"Great. You should receive your test results by mail in approximately six weeks." She handed me a business-sized card with a number and some additional information, "If you don't hear anything in six to seven weeks, call this number." She looked at me with a smile as she reached her hand out to assist the person standing behind me.

"Thank you," I said.

I spent the next six weeks patiently awaiting my results as summer turned into a balmy, Florida-style fall, and my daughter started her senior year of high school. Life was good; my relationship with Steve was blossoming. We were in love, and things were progressing quickly. We had booked our first trip as a couple to Key West in the early part of October. I was excited to get away with him for a few days and hopeful that the test results would be behind me.

Around the 4-week mark, I started anxiously checking my mailbox. I was feeling restless. To my surprise, the results arrived early. Standing at the pod of mailboxes at the tip of the block of townhouses, I couldn't bear waiting to walk home and read the results. I ripped open the envelope. My hands shook as I opened the tri-folded sheet of paper. It felt like waiting to hear who won the Oscar for Best Actress. I could hear the drumroll in my head:

language arts and essay, *pass*; science, *pass*; social studies, *pass*; math, *fail*.

The letter read: *To earn the General Education Development Diploma in the State of Florida, you must score at least 145 points combined.* My heart sank. I'd missed passing the test by five points. I kept reading. *You must retake the Math section in order to...*

Math. Fucking math, figures.

I had a choice. I could either let that hurdle keep me from the race or choose to keep training until I made it across the finish line. I could hear opposition making its case, but I made my counterclaim. I was stronger than the opposition; I wouldn't let a few numbers and formulas stop me. I refused to cry. Instead, I summoned my brave front and center. I demanded more from myself. I enrolled in a three-week, online GED math course, bought an extra workbook, and studied every morning and late into the evening after my gigs. I re-registered for the math portion and continued to keep my secret from my family, friends, and Steve. This was my battle to fight. I was standing on the front line of a mental war I had waged on myself for forty-three years. I was determined to overcome this obstacle instead of allowing it to bury me.

All was going well until I started coming down with severe chest congestion, exhaustion, and a sinus flare-up. My breathing was labored, and as an asthmatic, labored breathing was something I couldn't let get too far out of hand, or it could turn bad real quick. I spiked a fever, and the nonstop coughing made it really difficult to concentrate. I couldn't work (because I couldn't sing), and I had to take frequent naps throughout the day to feel better. I finally went to the doctor and was diagnosed with walking pneumonia. There was no hospitalization, but I was sent home with a cocktail of meds and a heavy dose of steroids. I was told to stay in bed and let my body heal with no distractions.

"If you have plans over the next two weeks, cancel and reschedule. No performing, no working, period. Stay home," the doctor demanded. "I'm not admitting you to the hospital right now, but I will if you don't take it easy. If you continue to have trouble breathing, go straight to the ER." His instructions were direct.

But I had a test to prepare for, and I didn't have time for a detour. I went home, started my meds, grabbed my books, laptop, and continued. I napped when I needed to and studied in between. My daughter was seventeen and could take care of herself and help me out when I needed it.

Little by little, I recovered. Although I wasn't near 100 percent and technically still ordered to bed rest, my appointment to retake the test was coming up. I didn't care how sick I was; unless I was in the hospital, I wasn't missing the appointment. I'd studied and felt confident in the material. I just had to combat the test anxiety. I had to remind myself that I was armed with the knowledge to pass the test I barely failed before.

It's only one section

One hour and fifteen minutes, that's all it was going to take. I was so close to the finish line.

Once again, it was test day—same building, same desk. I could do it. I could get through this roadblock. I still wasn't feeling well, and I'm sure I was driving everyone crazy with my lingering cough, sniffling, and blowing my nose as I recovered from walking pneumonia. But I would let nothing stop me.

And this time, when I read the results five weeks later, standing in the same spot as nine weeks earlier, the page told a different story: *Math passed. You have successfully met the requirements necessary to pass the Florida State General Education Development high school equivalency exam.*

At forty-three years old, I'd finally earned my high school diploma—I made it to the starting line. The possibilities were endless.

PART I
THE CLIMB

CHAPTER 1

Write like someone who's never heard of shame; write like someone who's been forgiven for being human.
~Glennon Doyle

~

I never belonged. I am the youngest of four children by twenty years and what my parents referred to as "the midlife mistake." And that is how I grew up identifying myself: a mistake. It was a running joke at every holiday gathering and family reunion. This was the first label I received; it became my identity and personal make-up. Family labels stick forever. There's not a scraper or chemical strong enough to remove the gummy residue it leaves behind.

My siblings were grown adults when I was born. My two oldest brothers, Larry, twenty, and Kenny, nineteen, were off to college and the Vietnam War. Larry was on a full football scholarship to the University of Miami, and Kenny enlisted in the US Army. Cindy, my sister, had just started her junior year of high school when my parents discovered they would have another baby. From the earliest memories of my mother's account, the news devastated her, which was never a secret.

As a child, I wanted to hear the story of "me." I think all children have that innate curiosity about how they were welcomed into the world. I wanted to know my parents' reaction when they found out they would have a fourth baby. Were they beaming with excitement? What was it like to hold me for the first time? I wanted to see pictures of my mom holding me, wrapped in swaddling pink blankets, as she lovingly gazed up at my father. I was eager to know everything. I can't remember my actual age (somewhere late elementary/early middle school) when I first asked my mom to share "my" story with me, but I remember her response.

My mom couldn't shake the flu-ish feeling she'd been carrying around with her for a few weeks. She was worried.

"I just knew I had a tumor. This feeling in my abdomen had to be cancer," my mother remembered. I'm not sure why, but I was expecting a somewhat more glamorous story. Instead, her comment hit me like a weighted punch. I felt the breath being sucked out of me with what felt like a heavy suctioned vacuum. I knew the outcome of that gut feeling. It was me, a baby girl: not cancer, not poison, not a death sentence—a *human*.

"Why did you think you had a tumor, mom?" I asked.

"Because, Jill, there was no way I could be pregnant. I was thirty-six years old—too old to have a child; I was using protection—the diaphragm."

I had no idea what a diaphragm was, so as a curious preteen, I asked. She explained that a diaphragm was to prevent an "unwanted" pregnancy. *Unwanted pregnancy.* The words reverberated in my mind. Another label: *unwanted.*

"Jill, because I was too old to have a baby. Listen, I already raised three children. Both of your brothers were in college, and your sister was finishing her senior year of high school. We were done raising kids. The last thing your father and I wanted was another child," she stated matter-of-factually.

As a middle-aged empty-nester, I get it, but I didn't as a kid grappling with belonging and identity issues. Not to mention, my mom was thirty-six years old. Although, back in the sixties, if you were over thirty-five, you were on the outbound train heading toward the second half of life, planning your retirement and pre-paying for a cemetery plot—not raising another child.

My mother's face was a hue of angst as her eyes rewound time. My heart sank. They didn't want me. That is how I felt at that moment. For many years, she told that story repeatedly at every family gathering.

After the doctor confirmed she was pregnant, she emphatically described her reaction, "devastated."

"Were you upset that it wasn't cancer, Mom?" I asked.

"No, but accepting the diagnosis would have been easier," she said.

I wanted to see pictures. Indeed, pictures would tell the story I so desperately wanted to hear. I was looking for anything.

"Nope. No pictures. I wasn't even awake when you were born. They put me to sleep. I was out. Don't remember a thing and didn't feel any pain. I woke up, and there you were." She said with a half-smile.

I learned to make a joke out of her devastation and my arrival from that moment. I did this to cope with the nakedness of the truth. I would tell that story repeatedly, even to my kids, and we would all laugh. But there's nothing funny about Becoming Jill.

Johnnie Mae

My mother, Johnnie Mae Woodcock (*yes*, that is her name), was the youngest of four girls (by twenty years) and had been shuffled around her entire life. Moved from sister to sister, home

13

to home. Her parents were "older and very poor, and had no room or patience for me," she said.

My Grandpa (John) Woodcock, whom I never met, was twenty years older than my grandmother (Mae)—he was sixty when my mom was born, and my grandmother was forty. They owned a small grocery store in historic Ybor City, Florida. Poverty-stricken, with no homestead, they lived in the back storage room with very little space for my mother. They shipped her off to her oldest sister Estelle where she lived for a bit. After leaving Estelle's home in Miami, she moved in with Phil, whom she always referred to as her "mean" sister and Phil's husband Fred in what was then a well-to-do neighborhood in west Tampa (about fifteen minutes from Ybor City where her parents still ran the family grocery store). Phil's husband Fred owned a successful parquet-flooring company, and my father, Jimmy Wilson, was one of Fred's employees.

Johnnie Mae, named after her father and mother (in that order), was a sophomore at Hillsborough High School and a majorette in the marching band. According to my mother, she was happy, though her sister Phil was extremely overbearing. Mom remembered the day she met my dad. Upon arriving home from school, my mom walked through the open-air carport, making her way to the side entrance of the house. When I asked her, she remembered that she saw a skinny young guy crawling down from a ladder with a rolled cigarette hanging loosely from the side of his mouth. She noticed how handsome he was with slicked-back dark hair, olive-colored skin, green eyes, and chiseled features, wearing a white undershirt drenched in sweat from the humid Florida heat.

"I stopped right in front of that ladder with my schoolbooks tucked under my arm," she said as she drifted off into a lifetime of memories. "I looked up at him, flashed a smile, and then extended a friendly 'hello.'" She acted out the scene like she'd just heard the director call out "Action!" Batting her eyes, pretending to hold imaginary books under her arm, flirtatiously, waving her long thin fingers.

As she made her way to the door, my dad made it to the bottom step of the ladder. His arm rested on the middle rung. "Hi, I'm Jimmy Wilson," he said and smiled as he tilted his head. My father also had a dazzling smile. I can just picture the moment the two of them locked eyes.

"Jimmy Wilson, I'm Johnnie Mae Woodcock, Phil's youngest sister." She hugged her schoolbooks to her chest.

"I know who you are," my father said.

"Okay, well, see you later." Mom turned on her heel and placed her hand on the knob, just about to turn it.

"Would you like to go out with me?" My dad asked.

"Well, maybe. I'll have to ask my sister."

My parents' first date was on Davis Island, a small island directly off the edge of Tampa Bay. My mother never said much about their courtship. The only evidence I have of their "date" is an old black-and-white photo of the two of them sitting on a seawall holding hands. The story jumps to dad's hard-and-fast proposal, leaving her with only two choices: quit school and marry my dad immediately or lose him forever.

My mother turned sixteen in the summer of 1947. According to her, she loved hanging out with her best friend Dolores and twirling her baton in the high school marching band. After a few months of dating, my father, a Detroit native, decided to move back north and take my mother with him. The only way she could do that, though, would be to quit school and marry him. Dad didn't care if my mother had an education or not. She would be his wife, give birth to his children, and he would be the head of the household: the patriarch. No wife of his would work. He was a man, and he was going to save her. No questions asked.

My mother couldn't stand the thought of losing her first love. I think in her mind, this was her way of escaping her childhood. This was her way of running away from a past of poverty and instability—of not belonging. She said my dad promised her the family she never had. He was her knight in shining armor, her way out. He could provide the proverbial American Dream. And in 1948, that's what was expected of a woman: a husband, children, and a house to take care of. She knew she could have all of that with him and was willing to give up everything to never lose anything again except herself.

Johnnie Mae Woodcock married James Emory Wilson Jr. on March 28, 1948. Their love story endured until my father's last breath on March 29, 2004, the day after their fifty-sixth wedding anniversary.

As I was growing up, my mom shared pieces of their life together. She told me the story of her first days as a teenage wife in Detroit. My parents arrived in the Motor City a few days after their Tampa nuptials. My mother, a Floridian, had never been out of the state and certainly never seen a bustling city quite like Metro Detroit. They lived with my dad's father in a small, run-down apartment. The day after their arrival, both men went to work, leaving my sixteen-year-old mother home alone with strict instructions from the men: "Do not leave this apartment. You're a young woman and won't be able to find your way around this big city."

My mother had no intention of allowing herself to be "put in a box," as she would say when she told the story. So, she decided she would venture out and find a job. They had no money; they were starting their married life from scratch. She wanted a home for the two of them, and that would require two incomes. So, off she went into the unknown to look for a job; maybe it was more about searching for her identity. She wound up getting lost until the wee hours of the night, but she was "never scared," she told me. However, she remembered that my father was livid. He established his authority—marked his territory. She never did it again. And she didn't have a job until many years later, just as my father requested.

My mother retold the story for many years to come, always with sass in her voice. Something in her eyes told a different story—a story she wanted her daughters to write but never gave them the tools to do it.

Although she was what I considered a free spirit at heart, my dad controlled her. And years later, this control would manifest in how she talked and treated him. I grew up watching her behavior and thinking it was customary to speak to your husband—or anyone that way. Not long after her heart attack at seventy-two, my father reached out to me and asked, "What am I doing wrong, Jill? Why is your mother so angry at me?"

"I don't know, Dad," I said. Until recently, it never crossed my mind that perhaps she'd been suppressing her anger and resentment toward him for the last fifty years of their marriage. Words spoken only through actions from years of control. She was constantly turning the other cheek for the sake of her marriage and society's constructs and expectations.

∾

James Emory (Jimmy)

My father was set in his ways—unrelenting, unforgiving, and harboring hate. He was the oldest of four and the product of an alcoholic dad and a codependent mother. Although my grandmother lived until I was in my early thirties, like most of my family, I didn't know her. I only knew the one-sided stories my mother told me. My father never said much about or to his mother. He never encouraged a relationship between my grandmother and me; that was normal because I didn't know any different. He seemed, though, to love and admire his father.

I never met my Grandpa Wilson. He died at forty-eight from a heart attack. According to my mother, my father would tell her he was a hard worker. But my grandfather was also an alcoholic and a very angry drunk. I've only seen one blurry picture of him in a white undershirt, tucked into his 1940s-style, single-pleated black trousers positioned just below his enlarged belly, anchored in place by a belt. He didn't look into the camera. Instead, I caught his profile with his index finger and thumb pinching a rolled cigarette. That's the visual I have of my paternal grandfather.

My dad never hid that my grandparents divorced and remarried several times when he was a kid and how "that just didn't happen back in the thirties." Divorce was like wearing the scarlet letter, especially for a woman. My dad would always tell the story of having to ride the cable car through the city of Detroit looking for a job when he was just eight years old.

"I had to quit school in the third grade to take care of the family. Your grandmother couldn't work," he said. But he never mentioned where his father was or why he wasn't contributing. I never inquired further.

The resentment in his voice was apparent. Yet I didn't hear stories of his father, and I didn't bother to inquire. My mother shared a different side of the story—of a man who was a raging alcoholic, abusive at times, "but a good man, whom your father looked up to."

In my childhood home, my dad's opinion was gospel. From his sports teams to his politics to the skin color he would allow sitting on his furniture, my father's beliefs were imparted to the rest of the family. Even as an adolescent, I knew something was wrong with that mindset. He hated anyone with a different ideology or skin color. They did not introduce me to any other side of life's story but my father's. The toxicity of patriarchy: Women and children should be seen, not heard. And that applied to me, too.

Ahh, the danger of a single story.

My father objectified women. He made sexist remarks about their breasts (the larger, the better), hair, nose, face, smile, and skin color. He loved the white girls on *Dallas* and *Dynasty* and the country singer K.T. Oslin. I thought sexist remarks were compliments, so that's what I looked for from a man. My brain didn't matter as long as I was "hot" in a man's eye and could use my looks to wrangle their attention. My dad used to make fun of my small, underdeveloped breasts. When I was twelve, my mother and I went shopping for my first bra. When we arrived home, my father brought out two Band-Aids and jokingly said, "Here you go, Jill. Your mom didn't need to spend money on a bra for you. These two Band-Aids will cover up your mosquito bites."

He looked down to the flat area of my breasts and laughed hysterically as he handed me the two Band-Aids. I tried to laugh it off with him and my mother. But inside, I was crying. I felt insignificant. If my own father didn't think I was good enough, what man would?

My father loathed strong, powerful women. He attacked their intelligence, but more so their appearance. He despised Jane Fonda. Her name was not to be mentioned in our house unless he was berating her for her advocacy. Gloria Steinem was another name that was not to be mentioned in our home and another woman I knew only by a name that connoted pure evil. I heard my father say time and again they were "disrespectful man-haters." A single story. According to my father, they were not "respectable women." He spoke poorly of women whose faces and platforms didn't fit his idea of perfection. To my father, women were subservient. My parents taught me to obey and fear the authority of a man. Especially my father. His sons, his grandsons, males: he favored all of them—and he was never ashamed of that.

BY THE TIME I was four, my two brothers and sister were married and starting their own families. I was too young to know or feel the resentment brewing between my family, but as I got older, it bubbled over like scorching lava waiting for the next eruption. The way I learned about the word "resentment" was not from a dictionary but from the actions of my family members who found me inconvenient. I was around seven when I first realized how my presence did just that.

Bedtime at my house was ritualized: Pj's, brush teeth, hug and kiss Dad, tucked in, and prayers with Mom. I was one of those rare kids that did not scoff at going to bed. It was the place I felt the safest. I got to talk to God. His presence through prayer was a protective layer around my soul each night. Even though I couldn't see it, I felt it. I would peacefully drift off to sleep, knowing the last conversation was with the One who created me with purpose. I held on tight to that notion. It's what's kept me alive.

One particular night was different, though. After brushing my teeth, I realized my parents were not in their regular evening position. I walked through the 1950s, one-bathroom, three-bedroom, ranch-style house and heard hushed voices hidden behind their bedroom door just off the kitchen. One rule of the house I never broke was opening their bedroom door when it was shut. But no one said anything about listening from the outside. I am not sure how long they had been in there talking, but the conversation I latched onto was enough.

"Larry is really having a problem with the lack of attention we are giving Lyndsey and Matthew. He says we are too old to have a young child and should devote more time to our grandchildren," my mother said.

"I'm not sure what he wants us to do about it, Johnnie. We have a seven-year-old; we are taking care of her just like we did when they were growing up. What are we supposed to do, give her away?"

Give me away? What does that even mean?

"I understand that. But he says his kids don't even know us and feel we give Jill more time, attention, and love. He says we spoil her, and she's turning into a brat. He predicts we will have our hands full one day if we don't stop giving in to her." My mother sounded worried, and I was having difficulty processing what she was saying.

Historically, my oldest brother Larry wasn't very nice to me. Anytime I was at his house playing with his oldest child (my niece) Lyndsey, who was four, fights would always ensue between the two of us. And it usually ended up being my fault. I dreaded our trips there because I never felt accepted. That feeling didn't go away until the day he and I made amends on his deathbed.

My dad responded, "That's ridiculous, Johnnie. I'm sure he didn't mean it. He'll get over whatever problem he's having, and things will be fine."

Let's just push it right under the rug and keep it there.

I quietly knocked on the door, scared to walk in. A hush fell over the moment; a single beat later, a verbal invite to open the door.

"Mommy, I'm ready for bed," I said. I hugged my dad, gave him a forced kiss, and said goodnight. Mom took my hand and led the way to my picture-perfect, pretty yellow bedroom with 1960s-style, lime-colored shag carpeting. I pulled down my daisy-printed comforter and crawled into bed. It was time to talk to God: "Now I lay me down to sleep, I pray the Lord my soul to keep. If I should die before I wake, I pray the Lord my soul to take."

Every night I would pray that God would bless them and keep my family safe. And that they would love me the way I loved them. I never told my mom or dad what I heard them talking about that night, and I never heard them talk about it or acknowledge my brother's actions again.

As a child, my parents gushed over my looks and raw talent as a singer and dancer. I was more a novelty than a little girl needing a sound foundation and shaping. My parents could take me out when they wanted to play with me, brush my hair, dress me up in pretty dresses, and put me on display. I was a natural-born entertainer. I loved being on the stage. My first dance lesson was at the age of two, and my first dance recital was shortly after I turned three. I sang in the church choir and never turned down an opportunity to grab a microphone and start singing. My parents loved that about me. My siblings, not so much. In their eyes, I was always trying too hard to be the center of attention, which only made the resentment grow stronger.

Growing up, more than once, my mother said that a woman's looks provide the best opportunities in life. My parents always told me how pretty and talented I was. Even though they'd say I was brilliant, the conversation would begin with my looks and "that pretty girls get the first dibs at everything." However, when I was twelve and in seventh grade, I went through a very awkward stage, as many middle schoolers do. My body started sprouting upward fast. I was tall and lanky, legs that went on for miles, just enough red hair to be the butt of every redhead joke, ivory white skin, freckles, glasses, and braces. I didn't look like the other girls, and I didn't fit in.

We had just moved to Brandon, Florida, a small town east of Tampa, from Toledo, Ohio, after my father was forced to close his struggling pre-stress construction company in Fort Lauderdale, Florida, my birthplace. Since the third grade, I had been enrolled in private Lutheran schools and was getting ready to begin the seventh grade when we arrived in Brandon, the town my mother despised. She hated the public school system, the people, and especially the idea of living so close to my dad's side of the family.

My mother referred to Brandon as "hick town" and wasn't going to allow her daughter "to grow up and become a redneck."

Perception was everything to my parents, especially to my mother. In the early 1980s, Brandon was a small farm town, primarily cattle and dairy farmers. I loved the place; I didn't understand what was so "hick" about it. I didn't even know what "hick" meant. The people were nice. People were happy. People were welcoming. It was a stark difference from the two cities where I had spent the first twelve years of my life: Fort Lauderdale and Toledo.

Although my mother hated the cold, she had forged many friendships up north and felt connected. She loved the community. It was the only time in my life I remember seeing my mom happy. I never heard the conversations between my parents when they decided we were moving back to Florida or the real reason why we left Toledo. Still, I clearly remember when we arrived, it was the beginning of a very dark time for our family (Mom, Dad, and me).

Living in Brandon, she often said she felt removed from everyone. As I remember, she was never happy and would comment about needing to get away with only my father or how lonely she was and how she had no one. I didn't understand how she could feel lonely. Our family was there, and we used to have a lot of fun at my Aunt Jean's house, which was only a few miles from our rental home. I didn't realize how much she disliked my father's side of the family until I was much older.

At that age, observing my mother's behavior felt accusatory. I took her unhappiness as a reflection of how she felt about me. I felt like it was my fault because she was always unhappy, especially around me. I don't think my mother realized how much I wanted to be with her and subsequently how much I felt her pushing me away. She was always tired. Dinner was a burden to cook (even though she cooked nightly), picking me up from school was a hassle, but getting me to extracurricular activities was a joy. Because that meant she would have time to herself (or

23

with my dad). For as lonely as my mother was, I felt it, too; I became conditioned to the emotion.

We arrived in Brandon just before the start of a new school year, and I had high hopes of finally being allowed to go to public school. However, my mother quickly closed the lid on that idea when she discovered seventh graders were being bussed thirteen miles away to a school in what she considered to be in the "bad part of town." Which meant (to her and my dad) a lower socioeconomic area of Tampa with, in her words, "lots of blacks and Spaniards." She wasn't having it.

Growing up, my parents painted the picture of black and Latino people and communities to look and feel like something less than the quintessential, All-American white family. They tried to instill fear in me that having a different skin color or ethnic background meant different and dangerous, both unacceptable in our home. My parents were determined to keep me sheltered and isolated from anyone that didn't share the same whiteness. But what they didn't bother to pay attention to was how different I already was from what they considered "normal," even with my white privilege and ivory skin. And that's where the issues were rooted.

When we moved to Brandon, the local Lutheran school was still fairly new. My mother wanted me to attend a school that had "worked the kinks out," as she put it. So, we found another small private school close to the house we were renting. My mother enrolled me in Maddux Private School for my seventh-grade year. She told me I had to wait until the eighth grade to attend public school. I counted the days.

The time I served at Maddux was challenging. I remember walking into my seventh-grade class feeling nervous and awkward. Most of the students already knew each other from elementary school. I was judged immediately on my looks. I wasn't blond, brunette, or tan; I didn't look like the other girls.

No one wanted to be my friend. I tried so hard to fit in, especially with the popular girls.

The star of seventh grade was a really pretty girl named Sherri. I wanted to be her friend with the fierceness and emotion of a prepubescent tween. Everybody wanted to hang out with her —*why couldn't I?* I thought. She had the most beautiful shoulder-length blond hair. It looked like spun gold to me. She had a tan, something I longed for. All I had were freckles that I wished would run together so my near-translucent skin would have some color. And she had boobs. I was as flat as a two by four. She was everything I wished I could be. If I couldn't be Sherri, I wanted to be her friend. This girl and her posse bullied me terribly. I would go home crying every day, asking my mom, "Why doesn't anyone like me? No one wants to be friends with me, Mom. I hate that school." I wondered what had happened to all the nice people in town. They certainly weren't at that school.

"Well, what are you doing to make them not like you?" My mom asked as she stood in the kitchen making me an afterschool snack. She stopped what she was doing, turned to me with an annoyed look and accusatory hand on her hip.

"I'm not doing anything wrong. I'm just trying to be their friend." I said. I just wanted to be heard—to be accepted. To be believed and to belong.

"Just let it happen. Quit trying so hard. Maybe you shouldn't talk so much. You know you do talk a lot. You don't need to work so hard at making friends. Just be normal, and they will like you." She finished what she was doing, laid my after-school snack on the counter, and walked out of the kitchen.

Just be normal and don't talk so much, I thought. Okay. I'll try. And for the next thirty years, I tried to be normal. And little by little I lost myself.

The next few weeks at school I stood on the sidelines waiting for others to seek out my friendship. But that didn't work either. I would stand on the playground alone listening to the sounds of my class-mates as they enjoyed recess. The laughter, the screams of excite-ment, the pounding footsteps of kids running by as they kicked up the Florida dirt, and scrambled mounds of red ants through over-grown tumbleweeds. The sounds of preteen freedom escaped the four walls of the classroom. Yet, I'd never felt so confined in my life.

Like many middle school kids, it was a lonely time for me. The girls would laugh at my hair and my braces, while the boys would laugh at my long, white legs and skinny, flat-chested body. I began to hate everything about me, especially my outer shell. I went home and told my mom once again how I just didn't fit in: "No one likes me, mom, not just the girls but the boys too. They make fun of my skin, my legs, my glasses, the color of my hair. You name it, they don't like it, and they don't like me. No one is ever going to like me. I'm too ugly," I cried.

My mother rolled her eyes, "Don't worry, Jill, the boys will love you one day. With that straight red hair and those long legs, you won't be able to fight the boys off."

What about the girls? I want friends; why did everything center on what the "boys" would think of me one day? *What about today? Right this moment?* I thought. From that moment on, I decided I needed to change everything about myself.

THE FOLLOWING SCHOOL YEAR, my mother made good on her promise and allowed me to attend public school for middle and high school. I was so excited, and after the year of being bullied and feeling isolated, I decided I was willing to do whatever it took to fit in. Even if that meant compromising myself. First things first, I was determined to change my looks. The summer between seventh and eighth grade, my mouth full of metal turned into beautiful white, straight teeth.

The glasses had to go, too. I decided contacts would solve all my problems; however, at thirteen my mom nixed that idea. I begged her incessantly for weeks before school started, but she refused.

"Not happening. I don't need one more thing of yours to keep track of," she responded.

It was then I decided I wouldn't wear my glasses once I got on the school bus and out of my mother's sight, which caused all kinds of issues—specifically, not seeing the blackboard at school, which had a direct effect on my grades. My mother finally conceded. I got contacts, and I took care of them like they were a national treasure. There was no way I was going back to my ugly glasses that were as thick as the bottom of two glass soda bottles.

Eighth grade started out much better than seventh grade had ended. As most middle-school-aged girls do, I started to grow into myself over the summer. And the changes were noticeable. With a beautiful smile, contact lenses to take place of the glasses, makeup to hide the freckles, a darker shade of hair color to cover the natural red, and designer clothes (skin-tight Gloria Vander-bilt and Jordache jeans along with the proverbial Members Only jacket) as my armor. I would do anything to cloak the "real" me. I wanted to look like all the other girls. I wanted to be popular. For me, that meant following the crowd. I decided to start smoking; it was a cool thing to do. If I was cool I would belong.

It was the evening of our middle school talent show a couple of months before the end of my eighth-grade year. A few friends and I decided that we would sneak out, find a hidden spot, and smoke; that's what you did in the 80s—a premeditated operation. After our parents dropped us off, we went inside the large audi-torium and were instantly lost in the crowd. No one would notice we were missing. The anxiety was building, and I couldn't wait to get outside and feel free from the constraints of authority. Surely my parents were long gone by then. Once we made our way out the door we found a secluded palm tree nestled behind the large school parking lot overflowing with cars of proud parents and family members just waiting to see their talented offspring. No one would ever find us. As the palms clapped to the rhythm of the setting sun, I lit up. The smoke billowed from between my lips; I tried to inhale mimicking a "real" smoker. The pressure and burning in my chest signaled a reminder of my inexperienced inhales as I felt my lungs char with every puff. Five minutes later, my parents' 1979 white Cadillac Coupe De Ville pulled up. I heard the muffled rumbling and familiar sound of the brakes. I saw the taillights reflected from the asphalt just beyond the trunk of the slick luxury car. *How the hell did they find me? Were they following my every move?* Why yes, they were.

My father opened the heavy car door, placed his left foot on the cracked asphalt, and in one swift move scooped me up by my arm from the warm, grassy earth and slammed my entire body into the oversized, blue, crushed-velour back seat. The odor of freshly cut grass was quickly replaced by the lingering smell of cigarette smoke and the familiar stale, nauseating stench of vodka permeating from the rocks glass sitting in the front seat cupholder. My father didn't go anywhere without his glass of vodka. My stomach tied itself in a million knots. I knew the rest of the evening would not be pleasant, but as a thirteen-year-old trying to fit in, the real horror was the scene my father made in front of my friends that night; however, that was only a preview of what was to come.

When we arrived home, my father banished me to the family couch. He walked into the large open kitchen that still smelled of meatloaf and mashed potatoes from dinner a few hours earlier, opened the cupboard door, and rustled around with the pots and pans. When he found what he wanted, he threw my mother's heavy, cast-iron, Dutch-oven pot at me.

What does this pot have to do with me sneaking out of the talent show and smoking? I thought to myself.

My mother was sobbing, standing beside my father with her head in her hands like I'd just committed grand larceny. Oh, the drama. My father walked out of the room and reappeared with his prized Canon 35mm, multi-lens camera. Dumbfounded by all that was going on, I then realized, for this punishment, there would be no physical beating; I would be subjected to my dad's favorite pastime: humiliation. My father reveled in humiliation. He was ready to focus his lens on my teenage troubles by telling an untruthful version of the evening's events through photos. With his camera in one hand and manipulating the lens with the other, he demanded the props I use and the way to pose for his shots. It was a full-on photoshoot.

"Take the pack of cigarettes out of your purse and start smoking. Smoke every last one of them as you look at the camera. I want your brothers and sister to see who you really are. The pot is for you to puke into after you've smoked that entire pack. Proof of what we are dealing with when it comes to you."

His actions spoke in waves and riptides, carrying me down to depths where I could no longer yell for help.

I was thirteen years old and a severe asthmatic. My father decided to torture me, sending me to the edge of a life-threatening asthma attack to punish me for being somewhere I wasn't supposed to be and smoking cigarettes.

"Smoking is bad for you," he said. "This ought to teach you." My father did not bat an eyelid. He took the photos, I smoked the entire pack of cigarettes, threw up, and then cleaned the pot, just as my father demanded. I recently discovered my siblings never saw the photos. It was all a messing of the mind. My thirteen-year-old mind.

My mother continued to cook from that Dutch oven for years following the smoking incident. I could never quite stomach any meal from that pot. When she passed away, that was the first thing I got rid of.

I didn't belong in that family—I brought shame to my parents, who thought humiliation and physical abuse taught vital life lessons. Who I was didn't fit into the square idea of their picture-perfect daughter. Every time I misbehaved or got into any trouble it was broadcast to the rest of the family like the evening news. Everyone knew all the trouble I was causing my parents. Especially my sister; they were very close. No one asked my side of the story. I was a child, only seen and not heard. They got to know me through my mother's stories and interpretations. From there, they made their judgments. Shame and hatred raised me.

CHAPTER 2

It's important for women to learn from our experience; not necessarily our happy experiences, but from the painful ones. When you transform your experiences into meaning or art, you've taken the process and used it in creation. If you are able to do that, you say, 'Thank God I had an unhappy Childhood!'
~Ellen Burstyn

*M*y mom's love was packed with conditions that underscored the dictatorship of my father. To add to the long list of dysfunction, both my parents were alcoholics. My father handled stress by drinking daily handles of Popov vodka; my mother dealt with stress by screaming, accompanied by drinking cheap wine during the week and always Bloody Mary Sundays.

The bridge between middle and high school was filled with much disquietude. I fought against my parents like a feral cat fighting its captor. In their eyes, I was a troubled teen. In my eyes, I never belonged. I looked for love and acceptance at every turn.

As I grew into a full-fledged teenage girl, I looked for that love anywhere I could find it. I thought I found it with my first boyfriend. Instead, I experienced physical and mental abuse that I substituted for love and an escape route throughout our involvement. I was desperate to evade the pain of not belonging.

I met my first boyfriend, Manuel, in Anatomy and Physiology at the beginning of my junior year of high school. He was everything my parents, especially my father, hated. If you weren't white, you belonged to a different caste system. "Otherness" wasn't humanness in my father's eyes. Manuel was a senior, nearly eighteen, and Puerto Rican. God, I was in love; I ran fast and furiously away from my father, straight into Manuel's arms. After years of being told by my parents that I was trouble, all I desired was to be told I was special. I had grand illusions and fantasies of what love felt and looked like. He was my first of many: my first love, my first sexual encounter, the father of my first pregnancy, and eventually responsible for the first of many beatings by a lover that I would endure throughout my life. When you haven't been shown unconditional love, the curious lens you look through is blurred.

My junior year of high school was tumultuous. I was in full rebellion mode at home and tired of the threats and humiliation. Admittedly, I was not an easy teenager to deal with. I was disrespectful, lied, and manipulated. But those were the skills I was equipped with. My childhood was grounded in manipulated threats. I learned from the best and became an expert in the field.

It was during the time of my courtship with Manuel that I dropped out of high school. Academically, I was barely hanging on to my junior status. Between my failing grades, chaotic home life, constant battles with my parents about my grades, boyfriend, clothes, hair, makeup, my future, and my attitude, I wanted to escape my life. At sixteen, I thought quitting school and getting a job was the answer (hint: it's not). I also thought Manuel would sweep me off my feet and rescue me. Oh, how I needed rescuing

—but mostly from myself. I needed my mom, not a boy. I needed guidance, direction, and love. I needed a female role model.

~

MY PARENTS FORBADE me to see Manuel, and I didn't care. I snuck around, lied to my parents to feel love from someone—to feel love from a man, something I felt little of from my father. Manuel and I were close, and we would not stop seeing each other. With a rebellious attitude, things escalated quickly at home. My mother and I were fighting. I was lashing out, disrespecting her, calling her names. And she would beat the shit out of me. With every fight, she'd call my grown sister and report my deplorable behavior—I'd hear her crying on the phone: "I just don't know what to do, Jill is out of control. Life is miserable. I didn't sign up for this."

She didn't sign up for this. *Neither did I, I* wanted to tell her. Those inflated stories spread like wildfire, and my mother was the arsonist. They were devastating to the future of our family.

At sixteen, I started dreaming of a family of my own. I would treat no human the way my family treated me; I just wanted to feel loved. Manuel's parents were always working, so his house, his bed, was our sanctuary. It quickly became my safe place.

I lost my virginity at sixteen. Physically, it was awful. Emotionally, Manuel took care of my heart like no one ever had. For me, the act of sex equaled love. I wanted more. I wanted him, and he wanted me. We had sex every chance we got; it was the only time I had someone's complete attention, and I wasn't going to give that up. He taught me how to do things I'd never heard of and although I wouldn't experience my first orgasm until many years later (and not from him); I pleased Manuel, and that pleased me. From a very young age, I was taught to serve a man—that's how you keep him. We continued to date; I frequently skipped school, and my grades were failing. My parents were losing hope and control; they were also becoming more mentally and physically abusive by the day. That's how they parented. The abuse from my parents ended with a beating, and eventually, everything stripped away.

Finally, when I came home from school with more failing grades and a manila envelope full of shame, my father looked at me and said, "You might as well quit school, Jill. You're failing, and you'll never be able to pull yourself out of this one." They gave up on me. I gave up on myself, and a week later, my mother and father signed the papers permitting me to drop out of high school.

"You want to be an adult? Then you will work like one. If you don't have a full-time job by the end of this month, I will kick you out of the house," my dad said.

Promise?

Although my parents allowed me to quit school, they were hell-bent on making life as miserable as possible. I was alone in a house suffocating in anger, disappointment, resentment, and shame. Work and Manuel were my sanctuaries. My parents and I clashed at every turn, and I was not easy to deal with. But what were they trying to teach me? Their actions spoke of hate and disgust, and I reciprocated their behavior. Little by little, I crawled into the empty spaces of my core searching for something that resembled happiness and normalcy. But what was happy? What was normal? Where did I belong? I had no idea, and at a time when a young girl should be shaping her identity, mine was floating somewhere inside of nothingness.

WITHIN A WEEK of my father's threats and demands, I landed a part-time job that quickly turned full-time. I worked weekends as a customer greeter at a local car dealership and receptionist during the week. I loved my job. I had visions of my parents telling me how proud they were that I was working; I did what they asked, after all, but that never came to fruition. It didn't matter what job I did or didn't have; home life was as miserable as it had ever been. Nothing, it seemed, satisfied them. I couldn't wait to get to work every day. Not only because I felt like an "adult" but because I escaped the reality of my dad's drinking and my mother's yelling (and drinking).

Despite my father's non-negotiable rule that I stop seeing Manuel, we secretly continued to date. However, the dynamic between us changed. He became very jealous and possessive. After I dropped out of school, Manuel could no longer keep tabs on me, and he didn't like me working. We had to sneak around to see each other, making things even more difficult. Between the two men in my life, my father and my boyfriend, I couldn't please either. But I needed both of them. I was taught to bend even when it broke me.

For most teenage girls, this is way out of the ordinary. Still, for me, already being conditioned to mental and physical abuse at the hands of a man (my father and oldest brother, Larry), it felt as routine as brushing my teeth each morning. I ran straight from an abusive home to the bed of my abusive boyfriend. The distinction between abusers was that one ended in a mental and physical beat down, and the other ended with sex. In my mind, Manuel's love wasn't abusive because physically it felt good. And at the beginning of our relationship, there weren't any welts left behind.

NOT ONLY WERE dynamics shifting in my relationship with Manuel, but the tension between my parents and me was growing. They tried their damnedest to keep tabs on me; however, in the 80s there wasn't the tracking technology there is today, nor did we have a security system in the home. My father considered himself the only "security" our family needed. But as a sober teenager living with alcoholic parents, I knew that once they were asleep, they wouldn't wake up easily.

Most nights after my dad finished off multiple servings of vodka (my mom a bottle of wine), and I made sure they were sound asleep, I would walk right out of the pool bath door that was attached to my bedroom, which led to the chain length fence that I'd jump. I'd climb straight into my boyfriend's car, arms, and backseat and out of my life. It wasn't for the proverbial tryst with Mad Dog 20/20 or the swift toke of a blunt: it was for the moments of physical love, even when the love was demanding and contentious, emotionally painful, and unaccommodating. I was sixteen, Manuel's touch was dopamine inducing. The flight or fight war zone that was a constant in my life was at peace. I drifted into those moments like waves gently lapping against the shore: release, pleasure, then again. I'd close my eyes and just be. A place I quickly came to long for.

As the weeks dragged on, tension built like a poorly constructed bridge ready to collapse. I'd go to work, come home, and go straight to my room. I tried to avoid my parents, but they were hellbent on forcing me to endure their resentful treatment at every turn.

"If you live in this house, Jill, by God, you will be a part of this family," my mother would yell through my bedroom door, over the blaring 80s pop tunes as I did my best to escape the bitterness that was home. "Turn down that goddamn stereo and get your ass out here." Most of the time, I only heard bits and pieces of what she was saying as I allowed the ambient music to drown out the voices of my reality.

Eventually, I appeared in the "family" room. My father would look up from his chair, glasses sliding down his nose, vodka swirling in his cloud-stained rocks glass, making his demands, "Go help your mother get dinner on the table. Earn your keep since you are living here rent-free."

I looked at him with an air of subversion that he caught onto immediately; I did not utter a word. I knew the response he expected. And I knew my actions would infuriate him. But I didn't care, which, in that very moment, far outweighed the repercussions. He ripped his glasses off the bridge of his nose, slightly catching an earlobe, as he demanded a military response from me through clenched teeth: "I didn't hear you, brat. I said go help your mother get dinner on the table."

I didn't feel like letting him win. Once again, I ignored his insistence and walked toward the kitchen. Within seconds of my obstinance, I could feel my father's presence creep up behind me.

"Jill Suzanne. Stop. Turn around. Answer me with respect before I slap you back to reality."

"What?" I asked, emphasizing the *t* at the end of my staccato answer.

My father raised the back of his hand only inches from the side of my face. His lips were drawn in so that only the bottoms of his yellowed teeth peeked through. His breath reeked of rotted remnants of his evening love affair with vodka. The smell sickened me. I hated him. I hated my father.

Those moments brought my crushing reality front and center. My rebellious streak ended. Not because I respected my father, but because I feared for my life. The back of his hand, which I'd experienced before, had the physical ability to knock me to the ground, but the emotional aftereffect lingered on.

I looked him in his glossy green eyes and quietly muttered, "Yes, sir." Bowing down to the almighty; that was how he liked it. He backed off like a lion satisfied with its prey, sat down in his chair, grabbed his watered-down vodka, and handed me the glass.

"Here, take this with you. Fill it up with ice. I need a refill. The bottle is on the bar," like nothing ever happened. The rage that penetrated through my father's demanding and abusive demeanor was at bay as long as I was saying what I was supposed to say and pouring him another drink.

My father's numbing came from his vodka on ice; mine came in the middle of the night when no one was coherent enough to remember I existed.

These familiar conversations happened almost nightly for weeks with the same scenarios, some more volatile than others. More times than not, they'd end in a yelling match between my mother and me, my father threatening to beat me or kick me out. My mother's reactions were predictable, yelling, crying, and threatening to leave because "she couldn't take any more of my abuse."

"Look what you're doing to your mother, Jill. You're killing her with your disrespect. She keeps threatening to leave and I don't blame her." My father stood eye to eye with my five-foot-eight frame. All I could do was blankly stare at him. I had nothing left. No smile, no spark, no identity.

One night he boldly threatened me. He pointed his leather-skinned index finger at the tip of my nose, "I promise you, Jill, if your mother leaves me because of your disgusting behavior, I promise you with everything I am, I will beat you until you are bloodied, until they throw my ass in jail for coming as close as I can to taking your life. I don't care. I will sit in jail and rot if you drive your mother out."

A clash of generations, mindsets, and patriarchal oppression intersected with deeply rooted teenage rebellion. A radioactive cocktail. Everything was bound to implode eventually.

A FEW WEEKS PASSED, everything changed, but not for the better. I was working, but my hours had been cut due to changes in management. My parents were putting pressure on me to find another job, but I didn't want to. I loved where I was working and had even considered selling cars, but wasn't able to because I was a minor. I depended on my parents for everything from the roof over my head to transportation, meals, and health care. They liked it that way, the control they had over me, always keeping me on the precipice of indebtedness to them. I rebelled, and they thought they could control me through manipulating mind games. And they did. I was only sixteen years old and certainly did not have the tools to be an adult, although I was desperately trying.

I wanted to get out from under my parents' watchful eye. Reflecting, looking at it from a middle-aged woman's point of view and a survivor of childhood trauma, I recognize that I, too, was manipulating and learned how to from a young age. I tried everything I could to break free of my parents' vice grip. I did everything they detested, purposefully. I didn't know what I wanted; I just knew I wanted out. I was emotionally exhausted: the drinking, the name-calling, the threatening tactics meant to scare me into "good behavior." I learned how from the best.

One Sunday after work, I pulled my dad's Datsun truck (he had allowed me to borrow it to get myself to and from work) into the driveway. I parked in the same spot I always did, under the window of my father's home office, but something seemed off. It was dusk and no outside lights were on yet. I gathered my things from the passenger seat and walked across the wide driveway to the open garage door. My parents rarely left the door open.

The atmosphere was heavy and lifeless as I entered the garage. Everything felt off—haunting. My mom's white Cadillac, their beloved car they drove for years, was parked in its normal position. The scene wasn't uncommon, but nothing felt right. The sun was setting through the rain clouds, creating a dystopian atmosphere. I choked on the overpowering smell of gasoline that lingered in the air as I gently ran my hand across the warm hood of her car. She must have pulled in not long before I did. I walked up the three-step staircase and entered through the large white door covered in years of greasy fingerprints and chipped paint into the laundry room. The laundry room, lead the way into the kitchen. The kitchen wore the familiar odor of bacon and eggs etched into the fabric of home.

I called out for my dad and then my mom, "Anyone home?" The big-screen television was glowing like the light from an extraterrestrial encounter, but no sound was distinguishable. I walked through the kitchen and into the family room. The space of our nightly altercations. My heart was beating out of my chest. I was scared. I wanted to run but was grounded in fear. Something was wrong. I looked to my left, and there on the 80s Formica eat-in kitchen bar, I found a note written in my mother's handwriting addressed to my father:

> Jimmy,
>
> I have left you. I can no longer deal with our daughter. She is nothing but trouble. Raising her has been the most challenging time of my life, and I can no longer do this. Something must be done. We must send her away. She is an embarrassment to our family and disrespectful to us. Once you have figured out what to do with her, I will consider returning. I can no longer live this way. ~Johnnie

I remembered the threat my father made a few weeks prior: he would beat me within an inch of my life and gladly sit in jail because of it if my mother left. I panicked. The fear and anxiety filled my body, and I needed to escape. Flight mode activated. I left my parents' home that day. I ran away to Manuel's, where I felt like I belonged. His family took me in. When my parents didn't hear from me for twenty-four hours, they panicked and called Manuel's mother who did her best to protect me. My parents told her what they'd done was just a tactic to "scare some respect into me."

"There's nothing left for us to try," they told her. Their plan was to manipulate me into thinking my mother had left my father, knowing that my father had made veiled threats a few days prior to the incident.

They demanded I come home but I refused. That was the beginning of a very difficult journey, one that lasted for many years resulting in terrible choices and decades of shame and heartache.

Although my parents could have forced their hand and legally made me return, they didn't. Manuel's mother asked them if I could stay at her older daughter's house. She lived across the street from Manuel and suggested some time pass for things to cool down. She assured them she would take care of things, promised them that Manuel would not be at his sister's house overnight. My mom and dad agreed to the arrangement but wanted me home in two or three days.

I did not want to go home; I was scared for my life. First, I knew that my being at Manuel's confirmed I had been lying to them about seeing him; second, I ran away, and that was something that was forbidden in our household. Growing up, my parents would always threaten that if I ran away not to bother coming back. I knew I would never live what I'd done down. They were forced to concede on their "rule"—when I caused them "worry" the world came to a screeching halt. They would tell me time and time again, "We have enough worry in our life, we didn't sign up for this."

We didn't sign up for this was a recurring mantra in my child-hood. To me, that statement symbolized the concept of unwanted. When a person feels unwanted, they are inherently pulled to leave a situation, environment, or culture that is toxic and solitary. The unwanted seek to belong at all costs. I found "belonging" with Manuel, and his family and I grabbed on tight.

Abused people do that, especially when they have been riding a raging current. And that had been my entire life.

From the outside of my own dysfunction looking in, Manuel's family didn't play manipulating head games. For the first time, I felt loved. And I was going to do everything I could to avoid going back home.

At first, Manuel filled the void of acceptance that I needed from a male figure. He filled me up. I felt hopeful when I was with him and his family. I wasn't giving up my relationship with him for anyone. His love was something I'd never experienced before. It was the closest to home my sixteen-year-old self felt. Although I didn't realize it at the time, it wasn't a healthy or fruitful love. But as an emotionally abandoned sixteen-year-old, it was all I had to cling to.

Manuel's sister, Nina, was a newly married young mom when I stayed with her. Her husband had joined the Navy and was away at boot camp, so my company was welcome. I adored his sister. She was everything in a sister that I never had. Nina and her baby boy lived in a one-bedroom single-wide trailer on the property adjacent to Manuel's house. She decorated her home with frilly curtains that hung from every window giving it a feeling of togetherness—something that I had longed for.

I slept on the couch for a few nights before I had to return to my parents' home. Manuel slept there with me. Although his mother promised my parents that her son would stay away at bedtime, there was very little supervision or enforcement of such. His mother pretended she didn't know, and his sister didn't care. She was happy to have the company, and at 21, 18, and 16, we were all kids, anyway. When Nina would go to bed, Manuel and I would do all the things high school teenagers were forbidden to do but that we'd been doing for months when I'd sneak out of my bedroom to meet him. We felt like grown-ups. It felt like we were wrapped in our own corner of the universe and no one could get in when I laid in his arms those few nights. I wanted that feeling to be permanent.

The biggest mistake we made was not using protection. We'd have sex and talk about our future. We came up with a plan that would completely change our lives. It was a solution that, at the time, made me feel whole and loved. In those moments of desperately searching for something, I felt like I belonged. I needed to belong.

My parents called Manuel's house and asked to speak with me. " We are coming to get you. What's his address?" my dad barked through the phone.

My mom picked up the other line. "Jill, we're coming to get you. Give your father the address," she demanded, echoing my father.

"Johnnie, I've got this," my father assured her, condescendingly.

As my parents demanded, I returned home. But I had some news and a request that only they could help fulfill. Three days earlier, the thought of going home was nonnegotiable. I was simply not going to do it. But with a plan in place, the one that Manuel and I made together, and then discussed with his mother and sister, the feeling of fear wasn't as marked. Knowing what I needed to tell them, waves of nausea swept over me. I was scared, but I promised myself and Manuel that I would know something by the end of the night.

My parents picked me up from Manuel's and we rode home in complete silence. The look on my parents' faces screamed defeat. It was like someone poked a hole in one of those inflatable yard decorations and all the air came rushing out, flattening the character like a pancake. There was no hug, hello, or relief that I was okay; the air was filled with nothing. I sat in the same back seat as when my father caught me smoking at the middle school talent show. Except I wasn't as afraid this time of what he would do to me when we got home. I was older and I could protect that little girl better than I could three years earlier. I'd learned survival skills over the years.

By the time we arrived home, something had shifted internally over the previous three days; strength oozed from an unidentified source. As my mother finished preparing dinner, I stepped into my bedroom; my once sacred space. The walls covered in Madonna and Van Halen posters, my beloved stereo and record player, a closet full of designer clothes, the waterbed I begged my parents to buy for me a few years earlier. I had all the "things." Yet, my pretty pink room and the 4000 square foot house felt like a hollow shell. I was no longer connected to its center or the family that lived inside. I didn't want those "things" in my room; I just wanted out. I wanted to go back to Nina's one-bedroom trailer, live on her couch with Manuel, and look at the frilly kitchen curtains that made me feel like home.

I took a hot shower and let the steam fog the mirrors and glass enclosure like a thick layer of dense clouds, so the reflection of myself was only an outline of the woman-girl standing in solitude.

"Jill?" My mother knocked on my bathroom door, startling me back to reality.

"Dinner is ready. Please come and eat with us." I could hear the tightness in her voice.

"Okay, I'll be right out," I replied. I turned the shower off and through the mist, I dried my dewy skin and got dressed.

Dinner was set in silence and took what seemed like forever to finish. I helped my mother clean the kitchen and, finally, we all moved into the family room. It was time to let them know what was on my mind.

"Mom, Dad, there's something I want to discuss with you," I said, as the TV filled the room with background noise. We were all trying to give each other a little space and not engage in a typical evening of chaos; however, I had a feeling that what I was about to tell them would light my father up. I was prepared for the fight of my life, which would more than likely end in a threat and some sort of violent behavior. I was prepared to run straight out of the house if the evening escalated.

"What is it, Jill?" My mother took her stoic gaze from the television and shifted it over to me. As confident as I was when I arrived home, sitting in front of my parents actually saying the words I intended to say was another story. I knew I just had to spit it out.

"Over the last few days, I've done a lot of thinking about things."

My father, trying to balance himself on his thigh over his hard, protruding belly, "Well, good for you. It's about time." I wanted to explode, but I held it together and allowed it to empower me to stand up for what I wanted.

"I know things are not good here, and I know you are really angry at me, Dad, and Mom. I know I made you want to leave Dad. And Dad, I know you love Mom and are angry at me for abusing her." I was determined to use his words to prove my point. "I think it's better if I don't live here anymore."

My father looked at me over the rims of his reading glasses.

"Oh really? Where do you think you're going to go?"

"Manuel and I want to get married. You guys don't want me here. I cause you too much trouble, and you didn't sign up for this." Their words, not mine. "Mom, you left Dad because I cause you so much pain. And Dad, you told me you would beat me within an inch of my life if she ever left you. I cause too much pain around here."

The room filled with silence, the kind of silence in a horror film right before the axe murderer leaps around the corner and beheads his victim. I was bracing myself for a couple of different outcomes, but I never expected the one I got. My mother chimed in.

"Jill, how can you say that? What do you mean you cause too much pain?" She had this concerned look on her face.

45

What the fuck? I thought. Did she not remember saying those exact things?

"Mom, you say these things to me all the time." I was growing impatient and frustrated. The typical gaslighting response: except back then, it was known as tough-love parenting mixed with a heavy dose of denial.

"Jill, they were just a scare tactic. We didn't mean any of them." She said this with all sincerity.

I about lost my mind. I was more confused than angry. The conversation we were having was like a prerecorded statement; rhetoric used to manipulate. Like I should have known that my father's threats were just a painful form of emotional abuse topped with fear-inducing panic attacks, anxiety, and rash decisions made by a lost and broken sixteen-year-old.

"I don't want to stay here tonight. Manuel's mom can pick me up after I gather a few things." I said as they blankly stared at me. No yelling or screaming, just whiteness. I couldn't see the curves and arch of their faces anymore; I had erased them from my memory and disconnected the emotions associated with my parents. They were just white slates. And all I needed was their legal permission to marry Manuel. I was experienced at disconnecting so I could survive.

My parents not only signed the papers for me to marry my eighteen-year-old boyfriend but attended the living-room wedding of their sixteen-year-old daughter. I was no longer their problem. I had a husband for that now.

CHAPTER 3

That room has been static for me so long: an emptiness. A void. A silence containing an unheard story ready for me to unlock.
~Margaret Atwood

The air between my parents and me was clouded with tension and tears. Every time I would talk to my mother on the phone she would cry. My father stopped speaking to me for the most part unless he absolutely had to. Their dislike for Manuel only grew by leaps and bounds. They hated him and the entire situation, but not enough to protect me from him.

Years later, I asked myself how I would have handled the situation with my own daughter. I'd like to think that I would have created a safe space for her even amid rebellion. I'd also like to think that I would have shown empathy toward her pain, even if that meant making decisions she would have hated me for at the moment but thanked me for in the future. I want to think I would have saved her from the outset instead of letting her drown in a bottomless ocean.

The truth is, I wouldn't have known how to save her. Just like they didn't know how to save me. I was void of the tools to parent. I didn't have a teacher, and neither did my mom and dad. Childhood trauma trickles down from generation to generation until someone has the wisdom to end the cycle. I thought by running away from my parents, I would be the one to end it, but that never happened.

~

AFTER THE "WEDDING," Manuel and I moved into a tiny apartment we could barely afford. We had no money, a few pieces of furniture, and not much food. Manuel worked as a fast-food employee earning less than $5 an hour, and I got a job at the ice cream shop next to our apartment. We shared a car, but I could never drive it. Manuel and I began fighting over anything that rubbed either of us the wrong way. The verbal fights quickly turned physical. He would slap me, pull my hair, punch me in the back of the head, and then seduce me. Sex, as it does so well, temporarily glued us back together. And it wasn't long before I became pregnant.

I was stuck in the middle of a ridiculous marriage, playing house, not wanting to crawl back home to my parents with my tail between my legs. When I told my parents I was pregnant, I knew they wouldn't be happy, but I thought it would bring legitimacy to the marriage, which was more for me than for them, I realize now. It did nothing but devastate and embarrass them and create more shame for me.

One afternoon, Manuel dropped me off at my parents' house on his way to work. We had agreed that I would tell my parents I was pregnant. They thought I was coming over for dinner.

"Mom," I said softly, "there's something I have to tell you." She was sitting on the porch drinking her wine, waiting for my dad to come home as she did every night. She looked up; the words from my mouth penetrated the dense air between us.

"I'm pregnant."

She stopped and looked at me. Her wine glass in one hand, she slowly placed it on the white resin table.

"What do you mean you're pregnant? I knew this was going to happen. Why the hell didn't you use protection?"

"We're having a baby, Mom. Can't you be happy? You married dad when you were sixteen and had Larry at seventeen." That's all I wanted.

The thought of being happy for your sixteen-year-old married and pregnant daughter is a lot to ask of any parent. I know this now. It's devastating to see your daughter making these huge mistakes. But I was following in her footsteps, after all. Couldn't she be happy for me?

Being angry and resentful after the fact doesn't solve a problem; it builds on it. I was broken, and I needed to feel loved and supported. I wanted it from my parents more than anyone—even after the tumultuous few years, we'd had together. I was always in search of their support. I wanted them to be proud, but that would only come on their terms, playing by their rules. Teenage pregnancy is complicated, but with the love and support of family, a person can get through anything. I didn't have that but oh, how I needed it. I needed them to show me how I could be proud of myself because I had no idea how to do it on my own. Although I wanted to be nothing like them, every choice I made was the example I grew up with.

"Jill. You can't have a baby. How are you going to pay for this baby?" She asked. "Does Manuel know? Just move back home. We'll take care of everything. You can have an abortion, and no one will ever have to know. We'll get you out of this marriage."

"Mom, I'm married. We are having this baby. I'm not coming back here. What would you have done if someone told you to abort Larry, or Kenny, or Cindy?" I said, leaving my name out of the multiple-choice question.

49

"If I had to do it all over again, Jill, I probably wouldn't have had children," she said.

One sentence told her truth. But not mine. I longed for a child: unconditional love reciprocated. Exactly what I'd been void of by my own family.

I was determined to make it all work. I was willing to take what I thought was the lesser of two evils: an abusive teenage husband and a pregnancy over living with emotionally abusive parents. I'd convinced myself the baby would make everything right and that Manuel wouldn't hit me once he saw our baby.

I can get through the next nine months, I told myself.

Financially, things got worse. I got fired from my job at the ice cream shop; I missed too much work because of all-day "morning" sickness. Manuel's next-to-nothing hourly wage couldn't pay the bills, and we were evicted from our apartment.

We moved into a small furnished apartment about ten minutes outside of town. This remote apartment sat back a few thousand feet off a two-lane country road between Brandon and Plant City. The apartment was a single extension to the home of a family I didn't know, although Manuel's mother had a connection to them somehow. They kindly offered us the place rent-free until we could start paying.

The walls were lined in wood paneling that soaked up the Florida humidity, making a deep cleansing breath nearly impossible. It was dark and dingy, but it was all we had. A perfect metaphor for the lonely and trapped space I'd gotten myself into. Manuel continued working the day shift, flipping burgers. I had no job, no transportation, no phone, and no one around. My parents made it clear that if I was going to have a baby and stay married to Manuel, I wasn't welcome in their home. There was nowhere for me to turn. My unborn baby and I were prisoners of our environment and the people surrounding us. This baby was all I had, and I would protect her till my dying day.

~

A FEW SHORT weeks after we moved out to the most secluded place I'd ever lived, I endured the beating of my life. Being spanked and slapped in the face as a child was something I was conditioned to. Verbal abuse, threats, and demands were equally a part of how I'd been raised but never had I experienced a beating like I did the day I finally left Manuel and the terrible choices that landed me in that position to begin with.

After coming home from work one afternoon, Manuel and I had a terrible fight over food, which we couldn't afford much of. I was two months pregnant, sick, and hungry. I'd been sitting alone in a dank apartment all day with no phone, TV, or any way out. I had no way to reach anyone. The fight escalated quickly, moving from the apartment into the dense woods that hugged the parameter of the apartment. He beat the shit out of me, and I ran as fast and far away from him as possible. I was in flight mode, a familiar place for me. There wasn't a tear in my eye, just a will to survive pulling me into its gravity.

I ran to the house at the front of the property but remembered no one was there. I knew I could never go back to that apartment or Manuel. I had to find a phone. I had to call my mom. With no shoes or identification, I walked about a mile east until I found the next house on that desolate county road. They were kind enough to let me call my mom.

"Honey, do we need to call the police? I think we should; you look injured," the elderly lady said.

"No, ma'am. I just want my mom." The tears I'd suppressed broke free. I couldn't recognize the sounds that were coming so deep from within. I tried not to worry the lady.

She handed me the phone, and I dialed as my hands shook like I'd overdosed on high octane coffee, when in fact, I had had nothing to drink (or eat) but water all day. The ringing through the phone's receiver sounded more like a drum roll as I anticipated a human voice to pick up. The answering machine was off, and I was praying they'd answer the phone. I didn't know what to expect. I was scared my mother wouldn't come and get me.

"Hello?" On the other end of the line, my mom's voice shook me to my core. Its familiarity broke me.

"Mom? I need you." I cried uncontrollably at the first sound of her voice—the voice of my mommy. In an instant, I reverted to the childhood I was robbed of.

"Where are you, Jill? What is going on?" The worry in her voice, as opposed to anger, surprised me.

I told her where I was, and within thirty minutes, she picked me up and took me back to the place I called home.

I did not receive a warm welcome when I arrived, not that I expected one. My father was angry at my mother for rescuing me. I never heard them fight unless they were fighting over me. And that night, they fought over me.

With voices raised, my father said, "Why the hell did you rescue her? She needs to learn to take care of herself. We've rescued her enough. She's pregnant; she's on her own."

"Jim, she's sixteen. We can't just send her out on her own."

"Like hell, we can't," my father replied.

"What is it that you want me to do?" My mother asked out of desperation.

"She's not living here, under our roof, knocked up with a half Puerto Rican baby. She will not bring any more shame to this family or us. Enough is enough—she's trouble. We don't raise kids that get mixed up with colored people, get married, and pregnant at sixteen. She's got a husband; let him take care of her."

I was stranded on a deserted island—physically and emotionally abandoned. Everywhere I turned felt like deep water surrounding me and no life preserver in sight. I was helpless. I was carrying a child that I didn't know how I would take care of, yet I already loved like a little girl who loves her favorite doll. I needed my mom, just like my unborn baby needed me.

The following day came quickly, and I knew I had to face my parents. I walked out of my bedroom and down the dark hall; I noticed suitcases by the front door. My parents greeted me with a command. "We have something to talk about," my mother said.

"Yes ma'am," I replied. All night I had been strategizing how to talk them into accepting this baby. I had a brilliant plan, and it would unite us as a family. Yes, this baby would be the catalyst for peace. I would show them what a great mother I could be.

I was bruised up, battered, and sore from being beaten the day before. My father looked at me, "Is this what you want? Is this how we've raised you to take this behavior from a man?" He said.

I wanted to say *you all do a damn good job of hitting me, too*, but I didn't dare. Instead, I responded the way I knew he wanted me to respond, "No sir, it's not."

"Let me tell you something, Jill. You are not having this baby. You will get rid of it and your husband, too. You'll play by our rules now."

"Daddy, please, please don't say that. This can all work out," I cried and pleaded, devastated by his words.

"This is not up for negotiation, Jill—"

My mother interrupted, "Jimmy, maybe we can talk about this a little more. Jill is upset. Her hormones are all over the place—"

"Johnnie," he said and looked her dead in the eye, "we are not raising another baby. We are not going to have another Jill. Our daughter can't take care of herself. How is she going to take care of a child? You'll be stuck with another unwanted child."

Another unwanted child, he said. Who was the first unwanted child? Larry? Kenny? Cindy? The unwanted child they are referring to is me. I was unwanted by my parents: there's no room for any more of my DNA.

As I sat with my parents, beaten and pregnant, my mother began to cry and excused herself, "Oh, Jill, why, why do you do these things to us? Why do you put us through this? You've caused so much embarrassment to this family." As my dad tried to comfort her, she left the room.

Not once did they ask if I was okay.

My father looked at me, "You never learn, do you? Haven't you done enough damage to this family? Haven't you broken your mother's heart enough times? You're lucky she came and got you; if I had answered the phone, I'd have let you sit there and figure it out."

I stared into the blank space of the room as I thought about what I was going to have to do to survive. I detached myself from the moment. As the day went on and things calmed down, my parents spoke to me again.

My mother looked at me. "You have a few options, Jill. First, your father will have your marriage annulled. You will either put your baby up for adoption, or you will have an abortion; however, if you choose to stay married and keep the baby, here's $100, the rest of your things are packed and waiting for you at the front door. That will be the end of our relationship with you —your choice. You will not embarrass this family any longer. No one knows you are pregnant, and I don't intend to tell anyone."

She explained that if I chose to put my baby up for adoption, I would be living at a home for unwed mothers for the duration of my pregnancy. They would tell everyone I went away to study. If I chose abortion, the nightmare would be over, and "no one ever has to know." And if I decided to have the baby, I'd be on my own or back with Manuel—they wanted nothing to do with me or their grandchild. I thought about my choices all night, and finally, I chose adoption. That was until I visited the place where I would be living.

WE PULLED up in front of an old bungalow-style home in a quiet south Tampa neighborhood lined in oak trees whose roots cracked the cobblestone road. I looked around, sick to my stomach, not sure if it was from my pregnancy or the stress of having to make a decision that would impact my entire life.

"Let's go," my mom said. "They are expecting us."

I slammed the car door and followed my mother inside. The extensive wrap-around porch reminded me of the houses I'd seen in the movies, a place where families would gather together fanning themselves, drinking iced tea, and reminiscing. This porch didn't scream togetherness or family. It felt severed. It was a porch where a young, pregnant girl walked in growing a human and left with nothing but fractured pieces. She went in a mother and came out empty and alone.

My mom looked around, making undecipherable comments under her breath. I couldn't tell if she approved or if maybe this visit would change her mind. With every step closer to the front door, I silently prayed she would turn around, grab my hand, and tell me she would help me raise the baby. That never happened.

As we entered through the front door, the house mother welcomed us, and we started the tour. I didn't hear a word the woman was saying to my mother and me as I looked around in a mixed state of panic and fear—traces of soured bile burned my throat as it traveled upwards through my esophagus, landing on my taste buds.

Get me the fuck out of here.

One girl was mopping, another dusting. The background noise from the TV room off the foyer was a low hush, just loud enough to draw my attention to the two very pregnant teens who looked like they were sitting around waiting for their baby to be born just so they could give it to someone else. There were nine girls total in various trimesters of their pregnancy. I would make ten. Everything was in black and white, a stark vision of sadness. Only the house mother was smiling. She reminded me of a car salesperson trying to meet their quota for the month.

The house was five bedrooms and two baths. Three girls to a room, and they all shared a bathroom.

How the hell do nine pregnant girls all share one bathroom? I pee every five minutes.

And the woman was still talking and smiling. And I still wasn't hearing a word she was saying.

I understood that if I moved in, my sleeping arrangements would be the twin bed in the largest (and only) room that slept four. One girl just had her baby, so they had an opening.

Lucky me.

I couldn't imagine carrying my baby for nine months and giving it to someone else to raise, and I couldn't imagine living there. Even though it was only a forty-five-minute drive from my parents' house in Brandon, I felt they would just leave me there until I had the baby. And maybe they would never come to pick me up.

Why does every room hurt so bad when I enter?

I was facing the toughest decision of my life. My mother pushed the idea of abortion, which I could scarcely imagine, but I also couldn't imagine adoption option either.

I was vulnerable. I was confused. I was scared shitless. I was sixteen.

"Mom, please," I pleaded as we drove home. "Please let me keep my baby. I promise I will be the best mother."

"Absolutely not, Jill. Your father is forbidding it, and frankly, I'm not up to it. I'm not going to get stuck taking care of another child. Especially at my age." She was fifty-three.

"Not to mention, if you have a baby in your teens, what man is ever going to love you? No one. No good man will ever want you and your baggage. You'd be marked a high school dropout and teen mother forever. How much worse can things get, Jill? No man will ever love you. You'll keep attracting the 'Manuels' your entire life."

She was right. For most of my life, I did attract abusive men.

But it wasn't because I dropped out of school and became pregnant.

"If you don't want to live through the nightmare of being shipped off to a home for unwed mothers and the pain of giving your baby away to a stranger, have an abortion. It will be quick and easy—*poof*. Your marriage will be annulled, and it will all be over. You never have to think about either thing again. We are willing to pay for everything and allow you to come back home where you are safe."

Safe?

I didn't feel safe anywhere; it was down to where I felt less afraid—the lesser of two evils.

A simple recipe for my mom. *Poof,* I could just get rid of it. And then I can forget about it, just like that. I couldn't imagine the pain of giving up my child, nor could I withstand the pain of domestic violence from my eighteen-year-old husband.

I couldn't sleep that night. Once my parents went to bed, I found myself in front of the two tattered suitcases still sitting at the front door; the $100 bill tucked in between the worn-out handles.

Where the hell am I going to go?

I curled into a ball on the cold tile floor and cried myself to sleep. I didn't think I could ever cry that hard again. But I did.

In desperation, stricken with the most profound fear and emotional pain that no teenage girl should ever have to go through, I decided to have an abortion. It was one of the saddest days of my life.

I CAN'T REMEMBER the details of the day. I blocked them out of my mind. But what I remember is waking up the next morning with blood-stained sheets and the worst cramping I'd ever felt in my life. I screamed for my mom, and she came running into my room.

"Mom, I don't feel so good."

She looked down at my sheets and saw the blood. "We're going to the emergency room."

Once we arrived at the ER, they whisked me back to a room, still bleeding heavily. I was weak and feeling confused by the blood I'd lost.

The nurse took my vitals and started an IV. "The doctor will be in shortly," she said.

The doctor came in, and Mom told him I'd had an abortion less than twenty-four hours earlier. After the doctor examined me, he said there were pieces of the embryo left in my uterus. They had to perform another DNC. I fucking had to do it all over again.

My body is empty.

So much for a simple procedure, and *poof*, it would be gone. That was their answer for everything for as long as I can remember. And then it became mine. For years, I learned to take the easy way out, to run away in the face of adversity. To detach, manipulate and lie my way out of everything and then pretend that it didn't happen. If it didn't feel good, I was out despite who I hurt or the consequences.

Today, I want to protect my teenage self. I want to go back and be the mother she never had. I want to hold her, stroke her long hair, and tell her she can't quit and that we'll get through this together with love, understanding, patience, and kindness. I want to tell her she matters and that I know she is hurting. I want to tell her she belongs. I want to take her by the hand and gently show her the future. I want to hold her in my arms and cry with her. I want her to feel safe, let go, and let it all out. I want to tear those high school withdrawal papers up, walk back to her classes, guide her, pray with her, touch her, care for her.

I want to give her virginity back to her, her innocence. I want to keep her from running into the arms of danger and give her the chance to love from the inside out. I want to put her broken pieces back together, every shard before they cause her to bleed out. I want to protect her—God, how I want to protect her from her entire world closing in on her and a future full of choices she didn't have the wherewithal to make.

I wish I could give her this gift of wholeness in her childhood, not as a parting gift from a lifelong scavenger hunt.

CHAPTER 4

The hearts of small children are delicate organs. A cruel beginning in this world can twist them into curious shapes. The heart of a hurt child can shrink so that forever afterward it is hard and pitted as the seed of a peach.
~Carson McCullers

*a*fter the abortion and annulment, I lived at home with my parents who were bound and determined to get me "back on track." I'm not sure what track that was, but they had a plan and handed down a new batch of ultimatums. To continue living under their roof and receiving their financial support, I was required to finish high school. I was too humiliated to go back to my former high school, not to mention I would have been two grades behind by that time, so my parents enrolled me in an adult learning program, or as my parents referred to it as "the school for drop-outs" in Tampa. It was an accelerated program, and I would be able to graduate not too long after my original graduation year.

I just wasn't into it.

I was still reeling from the emotional trauma of the past year. I needed to heal, but there was no time for that. And my parents wouldn't pay for counseling or professional help. According to my parents, I would heal as I finished school and worked. This was non-negotiable.

I attended the school for a while but ended up quitting again. The air was tense at home with my parents, and when I dropped out of school for the second time, they were ready to give me the final boot. Until the day my mom called me to her room. She had something important that she wanted to talk about. *Great,* I thought.

I wonder where I'll go when she kicks me out. I was bracing myself for another threat, ultimatum, and release.

As I entered my parents' massive bedroom, my mom motioned me to sit with her on her beloved antique, Victorian-style couch, which sat just to the side of their waveless (all the rage in the 80s), king-sized waterbed.

"Come, sit down," she gently ran her hand over the faded crushed velour cushion. Her voice was soothing, and for the first time in months, she smiled at me.

The plush white carpeting felt like soft cotton balls on the bottom of my feet as I walked across the room to her. A strong odor of chlorinated water was etched into the fabric of the space from the full-size hot tub that, for some reason, was in their bedroom instead of outside (weirdest fucking place for a hot tub).

I stopped for a moment. Mom's smile made me feel hopeful, loved, and protected. For years, I'd felt alone, unloved, and burdensome. The wall of isolation and resentment that my father had constructed between myself and my mom felt as if it was crumbling as she invited me to her.

"In this morning's paper, there was an audition notice for Busch Gardens. They are looking for singers and dancers of all types. I think it would be a good idea if you auditioned." It was less of a suggestion, more of a command.

I swallowed hard and looked at her. "I don't know, mom. I haven't taken a dance class in a few years, and I haven't been singing since I was in the jazz choir." I was not confident this was a good idea. Busch Gardens? Although that had always been my dream, I wasn't a professional entertainer.

"Oh, please, Jill. You sing in your room all the time! You've been singing since you came out of the womb." Somewhere between showing support and shaming me, she was convincing.

Singing with a brush in front of my mirror is different from actually auditioning for a professional singing job.

"Mom, no. It's a great idea but not a reality," I said.

She quickly interrupted, "It is a reality, and you're going to audition. You aren't in school, you don't have a job, and you are going to audition." There was no negotiating.

Once I wrapped my head around the idea, I was excited by the prospect.

Over the next few weeks, I practiced for my upcoming audition. My parents expected me to rehearse repeatedly in front of them as they played the perfect pair of armchair judge and jury. Finally, it was audition day. The fear disabled all rational thinking; I tried every excuse in the book not to go. My mother wasn't having it.

The audition was at the Old Swiss House, an on-site replica of a restaurant in Switzerland the founder of Busch Gardens had built for his wife in the mid-1960s. For years patrons sat amidst red velvet walls and Swiss cuckoo clocks eating dinner while looking out over the makeshift Serengeti. In the early 1980s, the restaurant closed and was used for theme park auditions and rehearsals.

The place was massive. As I looked up at the vintage architecture, the building seemed to stare back at me like an angry old man. The long set of stairs leading up to the massive wooden doors looked like its arms were reaching out to pull me into its grip and not let go. I did not get a warm feeling. I was seventeen and coming out of the worst few years of my life. I was unsure of everything.

As a little girl, all I wanted to do was sing and dance on stage. I began singing in the church choir and performed my first dance recital at three. Entertaining was in my blood. I took dance lessons: ballet, tap, and jazz starting at three years old and continued until I dropped out of high school (the first time). I loved it. Singing, on the other hand, just came naturally. I never took a voice lesson in my life; I just did it. I heard a song once and could perform it just like the artist in most cases. Growing up, my absolute favorite things in my room were my record player, FM radio, and portable eight-track cassette player. Like the way kids today are attached to their cell phones, that was me with anything music. If you took my music away, you took my life.

I spent years in front of my mirror singing, dancing, and giving my Grammy acceptance speech(es). But the thought of auditioning, being judged, was terrifying. I'd already spent the first seventeen years of my life being judged and rejected by the people who were supposed to love me; I wasn't sure I could take rejection from strangers.

Looking up at the maze of stairs was like standing at the base of a rocky mountain, not knowing how I would chisel my way to the top: I had the equipment but didn't feel confident enough to use it and make it to the summit.

I stood there looking up as my mother's patience waned. "Get your ass up those stairs, Jill. I didn't spend thousands of dollars on dance lessons for you to back out." She wouldn't let me worm my way out of this one. It was time to start the climb.

We signed in and waited. The room was filled with other singers and dancers warming up their bodies and voices. I had no idea what I was doing. I just sat there holding my breath, waiting for my name to be called. I felt like I was lost and had made a wrong turn down a dark, unfamiliar alley, not knowing if I'd ever make it out. I had no idea what an audition entailed besides auditioning for my high school jazz ensemble when I sang a rendition of an old Madonna song.

The wait to be called was a lifetime. After what seemed like years of sitting inside myself, wrapped tightly in self-doubt and insecurity, I heard my name. I looked over at my mother and slowly rose from the chair; I couldn't feel myself walk. I followed the large arrows printed on cheap printer paper, barely taped to the velour wallpaper. My legs took over my brain; instead of running away, they led me into my future and a large room filled with the people who would become my future mentors and life-long friends.

As the door shut behind me, it sounded like a vault closing. I couldn't escape. The audition team was sitting at a long table at the far end of the mirror-lined room. Behind me, in the corner, was an old upright piano. *Holy shit,* I thought to myself, *what have I gotten myself into? This is way out of my league. I don't belong here.* I wanted to snap my fingers and disappear like the characters in a sci-fi movie, but instead, I handed my sheet music to the piano player. He asked me a couple of questions—I can't remember my bullshit answers—and the next thing I know, I'm singing. I was all in. Willpower took over.

I was seventeen and loved 80s pop music. In my inexperienced preparation, I decided I would wow the judges with some of my favorite songs: the ones I'd been singing in my mirror with my hairbrush. Looking back, my audition selections (Tiffany's version of "I Think We're Alone Now" and the 80s bubblegum pop group Expose's "Seasons Change") probably weren't the choices of the other skilled and seasoned auditionees. But when I started to sing, I noticed the music director smiling and tapping his hands to the beat of the music. Since that time, Desmond Boone and I have become lifelong friends. He probably doesn't know this, but his big, encouraging smile and hand tapping gave me the courage to continue even though I felt like I was being swept offshore by an angry ocean undertow. His smile helped me breathe through it all.

Once I finished singing, it was time for my solo dance audition. I was required to choreograph my own number for the first part of the audition. Again, I had no idea what the fuck I was doing. But I was damn sure doing it. I made it through in one piece. When I was finally done, I felt as if I had just crossed the finish line of a seventeen-year triathlon. I rehearsed my entire life and gave the performance of a lifetime. I was in control. I felt the chances were slim that I would be selected to be a professional performer at a popular American theme park, but walking out of that room, I knew I would do it again and again until I made it. I was empowered. I used my talents to do something I'd only dreamed about my entire life. And for whatever her M.O. had been, my mom had encouraged me to follow through with what she knew I was capable of.

As I was exiting the audition room, they asked me to wait. I slowly turned around. One of the women sitting next to the happy gentleman tapping his hands, Donna Bachem, better known as "B," as I've called her since that day nearly thirty-five years ago, asked me to please return for the group choreographed dance. My callback. I was beyond excited, and I felt hopeful for the first time in years. Mostly, though, I couldn't wait to tell my mom. I knew she would be proud of me.

I ran out of the audition room, straight to where she was sitting. I stood in front of her, "I got called back! I have to come back for the group choreographed number in a couple of hours!"

She teared up. "I told you. Now, aren't you glad I made you audition?

Yes, I was. She never ceased to remind me, and I never thought to thank her. I made it through the auditions and was hired as a singer and dancer. I'd never seen my mother so happy about anything in my life.

Busch Gardens holds many memories for me and is not only responsible for my debut into the entertainment world and for fulfilling my dreams of becoming a professional entertainer but ultimately responsible for the beginning of my little family.

WORKING at Busch Gardens as a performer had its ups and downs, but I learned a lot from that time in my life, and it most certainly kicked off a nearly thirty-year career in the music and entertainment industry. Music saved my life. And I do owe that push to my mom. I would have never had the courage to go through with the audition if she hadn't insisted upon it. Although our relationship was tense for most of my life, she supported my love of performing. She bought season passes for the next two years and sat in the front row nearly every day on her way home from work. Once I was making a living, she supported me.

I worked at Busch Gardens for almost two years, and in that time frame, I met many wonderful people who, to this day, are still very good friends of mine. I consider some of these people my "lifers." We will always be in each other's lives.

MY SON WAS the best thing that came out of my time at Busch Gardens. I met Alex's father, Aaron, while working at Busch Gardens. He played saxophone in the band in both shows that I performed in. Aaron was eleven years older than me. Because of the age difference, I can't say that it was love at first sight; all the guys in the band seemed like grown-ups compared to my almost eighteen-year-old self. However, Aaron and I began flirting in between shows as we all shared the same dressing/breakroom.

We did four shows a day with a couple of hour breaks in between performances; there was lots of downtime for us to engage.

Aaron was the practical joker of the cast, which attracted me to him. He was also a musician; I had an affinity for musicians for years—there was nothing sexier in my mind. Aaron was established, owned his house, drove a sports car, and could take me to fancy places even though I was underage. And that he did. We started dating, and it was a whirlwind—lots of drinking, sex, and spending money. I was so young and fell in love so hard with him. The relationship was anything but healthy. I was a little girl, emotionally and mentally immature, and the last thing I needed was to be in a relationship with a chemically dependent and depressed man. I knew going in that Aaron had a drug and severe drinking problem, but being around addicts was something I was accustomed to. I grew up with a family full of them. It was normal to fight, yell, pitch fits, and manipulate. Again, this was my normal. We were both poster people for dysfunction, and we carried that dysfunction into our relationship.

Aaron and I had a rocky beginning, middle, and end. We dated off and on for two years, mainly because I inserted myself into his life even when he tried to tell me things would never work out. I was bound and determined to marry him. My parents loved him. They saw Aaron as someone who could take me off their hands even though things had gotten better at home since I started my job at Busch Gardens. They didn't care about the age difference or the fact that Aaron was an addict or that he was abusive both mentally and physically to me. They just wanted someone to take care of me, so they didn't have to. I guess I saw the same benefits in some respects, even though I was too naïve to sit with my intentions. To know that I was continually on the hunt for the next best man. A fairy tale ending. The one that never came.

Aaron could do no wrong in their eyes, and he was white. There were times when he would quit drinking and drugging, and that's when things were the best between us. I'd quit drinking to support him as well. We were the happiest we'd ever been. I moved in with him, and our relationship was shaping into a healthy one. One night, a few weeks after my twenty-first birthday, he pulled a little black box out of his pocket and proposed to me as we were lying in bed watching TV. I was ecstatic. And when I announced our engagement to my parents, I'm not sure anything could have made them as happy as hearing the words, "Aaron asked me to marry him, and I said yes!"

Aaron and I married on Captain Memo's Pirate Ship, complete with the pirate, parrot, and cannon (you can't make that shit up). We had a small group of family and friends gather for the celebration. I sang to Aaron, and he accompanied me on his saxophone. For getting married on a pirate ship, it ended up being a lovely ceremony. The following March, we celebrated our first anniversary in the hospital. I had just given birth to our precious baby boy, Alex, the day before.

Once again, I had no idea what I was doing when I brought my son home. No one had shown me how to adult or how to mother. I was blindly navigating through life, which was the only way I knew. Growing up, the example I had was the tumultuous and chaotic environment I was born into and the iron-handed, 1950s-style example of parenting I was raised by. Twenty-one years old, five-day-old baby, and no guidance, I was petrified and exhausted. It was like being thrown into a pool for the first time and being told to swim the hundred-meter breaststroke without any idea what the fuck the breaststroke was. But through it all, nothing made me happier than being a mother to Alex.

Although Busch Gardens was a catapult into a decades-long career in music, I'm most thankful for my son as a by-product of that time and a stark reminder that there are hidden gifts inside each of our life experiences.

～

I COULDN'T HAVE BEEN BLESSED with an easier baby. Alex was happy and healthy. I couldn't have had a better teacher "on how to mom" than my sweet baby boy himself. We were an inseparable team, Alex and me. My marriage, on the other hand, was collapsing. My husband was a full-time working musician. Before we married, I left Busch Gardens, but he continued his tenure at the theme park as he had since the late 1970s. In addition to performing full-time at Busch Gardens, he was also a gig player, meaning he freelanced with a variety of bands. Although his day job was Monday-Friday, for nearly a year, he played seven nights a week with a popular band in Sarasota, Florida—about two hours from our home—sometimes two gigs a day on the weekends. I never saw my husband.

This workload wreaked havoc on our marriage and took a toll on Aaron, personally. He was overworked and burned out. After a couple of years of sober living, clean of alcohol and drugs, Aaron returned to these substances to help him get through his busy schedule. To what end, I had no idea, until one night, I discovered just how out of control it had gotten. Aaron went to rehab, and shortly after that, our marriage collapsed.

CHAPTER 5

The struggle of my life created empathy...I could relate to pain, being abandoned, having people not love me.
~Oprah Winfrey

After our divorce was final, Aaron and I shared custody of our son. He had proven his sobriety, and from what I could tell, he worked the Alcoholics Anonymous Twelve-Step program into his life. My son and I moved in with my parents just before his first birthday and began to rebuild our lives. I worked in various bands as a lead singer, and my parents watched my son in the evenings. Aaron would take Alex every other weekend on his days off.

It wasn't long before I started dating again. I was single and twenty-three years old. Looking back, there were lots of things I would have done differently. That's the beauty in finding fifty: our regrets are loaded and dangerous; however, we need to discover how to shape them into something functional. I didn't know how to mother, and my son and my relationship paid the price over the years. I yearned for love and attention from a man, even at the risk of losing everything I had in front of me.

My relationship track record was zero for two. Living with my parents as an adult was a terrible choice but the only one I allowed myself to make. It didn't let me get out of my own way. I didn't know how because I was never shown how in my formative years. Although I went through a harrowing dysfunctional childhood, I disassociated from the memories and suppressed my own internal "that's the right thing to do" meter. I just barreled through the decades of my twenties and thirties like a bull chasing a matador. And that's what every relationship I had resembled. There was nothing organic about any intimate relationship I entered into. Nothing started slow—it was full-speed ahead or nothing. Especially when it came to men and precisely when it came to my daughter's father, Scott, and my subsequent third marriage.

I met Scott a few months after my divorce was final from Aaron. My brother Larry's daughter, Lindsey, studied at the University of South Florida and lived in an apartment about thirty minutes from my parents' house. I was a singer in a well-known Tampa wedding band and worked a few nights a week, mostly weekends, which gave me little time to go out with friends my age. Quite a few of our gigs were in and around various venues in Tampa, so occasionally, I would stop by Lindsey's apartment well after midnight for a drink and some socializing. Even as adults, Lindsey and I were not close, but we tolerated each other. She made it clear that her house was her territory, so I would tread lightly when I spent time with her inner circle. Her friends treated me better than she did and were fun to hang out with, so I did my best to ignore her and concentrate on the others.

There was always a party at Lindsey's townhouse and lots of people in and out of her place. The typical college living arrangement. Although she was a complete bitch toward me, her friends were cordial, and it provided a little bit of escape from my life. I was always trying to escape.

One afternoon, my son and I decided to stop by Lindsey's. She loved my son and I would sometimes bring him over on weekend afternoons (when things were quiet around her apartment), and we would hang out for a while. When I arrived one Saturday afternoon, our beloved Miami Hurricanes, her father's alma mater, were playing, and a group of friends gathered to watch the game; things were calm for a college football game. Everyone was tired and hungover from the night before. As I walked through the front door, I expected to see the usual gang, but there was one guy I hadn't met before. I was immediately drawn to his good looks—chiseled features, reassuring smile, olive skin, sky-blue eyes, and toned physique. He was easy on the eyes, and I wanted to know him. The introductions were made.

Although I was only three and a half years older than Lindsey, the title "Aunt Jill" was a running joke with her group of friends.

Lindsey, of course, made the introductions, "Scott, meet Aunt Jill," she said with an annoyed tone, brushing anything genuine to the side as her body language silently reflected a "don't even think about it" display.

"Aunt Jill, Scott. Stay away from him. I know that's a difficult task for you. But do your best." She sternly delivered her orders, with a side of humiliation, which was to be executed, or else I wouldn't be invited over again.

Scott stood up, looked at me, and said, "Hey, Aunt Jill," with a mischievous giggle and smile that stopped my world from revolving and my legs from moving. "Who's this?" he inquired of the little person pinned on my hip.

Our eyes met, "This is Alex, my son." I smiled and nervously brushed Alex's soft hair off his forehead.

Scott took Alex's hand. "Nice to meet you, dude," he said.

Alex smiled with his scrunched nose and gap between his two front teeth. He was such a happy baby, and it showed. He wiggled to get out of my arms as most toddlers do when they want to explore new terrain. I set him down, and immediately he diverted everyone's attention from the football game to his shenanigans. Scott and I stood there for a few minutes making small talk, but there was a connection: we both felt it. I could see Lindsey out of the corner of my eye sizing up the situation and not appreciating that I wasn't following her "orders" to stay away from him.

By October, Scott and I had become an item. We weren't quite a couple, but we were heading there. He was casually dating another girl, but it was obvious that there was a mutual attraction between us. One Saturday evening, I was over at Lindsey's, hanging out with the group. I stopped by after my early gig but did not plan on staying late because I had an afternoon gig the next day. As I was sitting on the couch drinking a beer and chatting with a few girls, Scott walked into the apartment, announcing he was taking "Kate" on a date. I looked up at him and couldn't help but feel jealous and wish it was me. While the others in the group cheered him on, I sat quietly, not engaging but smiling just enough not to give my true feelings away.

Scott looked over at me and asked, "Where do you think I should take her?"

"Wherever you want," I said.

"What are you up to tonight?" he asked and sat down next to me.

I felt the butterflies swirl in my tummy and a tinge of disappointment, knowing he was only minutes if not seconds away from walking out the door and going on a date with Kate.

"I'm just going to hang here for a bit and then head home. I have an afternoon gig tomorrow, so I need to make sure my voice is well-rested."

"Well, have fun. I'm not sure how late I'll be, but if you stick around long enough, maybe I'll see you when I get back." He smiled, looked around the room at his audience, and left.

I waited for a while in anticipation of his return but knew I needed to head home before it got too late.

About an hour after I got home, the phone rang. There was Scott on the other end.

"Hey, Aunt Jill. What are you doing? Why didn't you wait?"

"You were on a date, and I needed to get some sleep," I responded.

"Why don't you come back over?"

"What about your date?" I asked.

"I took her home. Now, come over."

So, I went. I had a built-in babysitter; why not? Again, not a good choice in retrospect. I arrived about thirty minutes after he summoned. We hung out, drank a little bit, and I got home around 4 a.m. There was just enough time to get a few hours of sleep before my son woke up at seven, and I had to work at noon. Scott showed up at my gig that day, and we officially started dating.

Our relationship escalated quickly. To Lindsey's dismay, she was unable to keep us from dating, but that didn't stop her from trying. She let it be known, out loud, that she disapproved. She did everything to keep us apart and tarnish our relationship, specifically by dragging my name and reputation through the mud. Scott didn't allow her words to dissuade him from pursuing a relationship with me, but the damaged foundation was set.

CHAPTER 6

We all have an unsuspected reserve of strength inside that
emerges when life puts us to the test.
~Isabelle Allende

"*I*'m pregnant," I said to my future husband, Scott.
"You're pregnant?" He needed to hear it again.
"Yes, that's what I said. I'm pregnant."

"I need to go to the bathroom." Scott walked into the bathroom and, with force, slammed the door, shutting me out.

I didn't know what to think. I stood there in our one-
bedroom basement apartment staring at the faux wood door,
wishing I could see through it to see what he was doing—what he
was thinking.

Does he have to pee? I thought. *Puke, cry, yell?* I heard nothing.
At twenty-five, I felt sixteen again, telling my mom I was pregnant, praying I wouldn't be rejected by the one person I loved
more than anyone in the world. The fear came rushing back like

a wave unfolding over soggy sand layered in sharp-edged shells. I was slowly sinking, feet first, into the earth.

This was an unexpected pregnancy. Scott and I had been dating for about a year and had recently moved from Florida to his hometown of Bloomington, Illinois. It was a significant change for this Florida girl, but I was excited to experience my first real winter ever—I just didn't expect to experience it pregnant. I was as shocked as Scott. I was on birth control pills and took them religiously. Scott and I even practiced the "pull-out" method, yet there I was, pregnant with my second child.

Scott emerged from the bathroom, looking as if he was about to approve or deny the blueprint of my life. I was desperately awaiting his reaction; after all, he did contemplate his reply on his throne: the shitter.

"Okay, let's have a baby," he said like I needed his approval—though, at the time, I needed it more than anything. I was raised to believe that a man's approval was the final say. I wanted his baby. Surely, he would love me back. The dark and dreary basement apartment came to life. The stuccoed white walls and the dingy popcorn ceiling felt like home for a brief moment. A place to love our baby and each other—a place that was a safe zone—a place where no one could ever take my baby from me. I found myself creating another fairytale, like the ones I read in books and watched on TV as a child.

"Really? We're going to have a baby?" I said, happier than I had been in years.

"Yep," he replied, "But you'll have to get a real job and provide your own insurance, Jill. We're not married, and we're not getting married anytime soon. I'm still in school, and I'm not dropping out."

"I'll do anything, Scott. I'll do whatever, anything. I hope it's a girl!" The smile on my face told ten thousand stories of hope. But the recklessness arising out of the desperation to be loved, to be accepted, silently sliced through and took over the reality of what was, for years, to come.

"Is this true, Scott? Is what she is saying true?" Scott's mother, Anne, demanded to know as we stood in her overly decorated, country-themed kitchen just a few miles from our apartment. As Scott leaned up against the shiny oven doors, arms folded at his chest, the right Michael Jordan tennis shoe crossed over the left; the narrative was quite different than a few short weeks before when he'd risen from his "throne," declaring, let's have a baby!

He glared at me through the eyes of an enemy. He hated me for telling his mother. Maybe he hated me for being pregnant. I'm not sure which of the two it was most, but I had to let her know. Inside the last few weeks, he quickly changed his mind about being a father. He wasn't ready, he said. He still had school to finish and things he wanted to do.

"I told you, Scott, I'm not having another abortion. Why is that an acceptable answer to you? We made this baby. I'm not doing it. We're 25 years old—grown adults. We're having this baby," I said.

"Then you'll have to do this by yourself. I'm not going to be a part of it." He was firm in his answer.

I had to go to his mom. Maybe she would talk some sense into him. Perhaps with her blessing, Scott would have a change of heart, and all would be right in our world.

"I'm asking you a question, son. Is this true what she says?" Anne demanded an answer.

He looked down at the spick and span linoleum floor and said, "Yep."

"How long have you two known this?" She stood with her hands on her hips. Her glasses reflected her son, who still hadn't lifted his head to look at either one of us.

After a few moments of uncomfortable silence, I spoke up. "About a month now," I whispered.

"A month," she said. "How did I not know this?"

"Because, Mom, we didn't want to tell you," Scott said, finally lifting his head to look at her—his arms still crossed at his chest.

"No, Scott. You didn't want to tell her." I said. He looked at me and walked out the garage door. He was gone.

Anne turned to me and said, "I'm sorry. This is not the man we raised him to be. But, hon, you can't have this baby. You'll have no help. And we're too old to take care of another child. You need to have an abortion and move back to Florida."

Again, there were those fucking words: I'm too old to take care of another child and abortion. Hell no, I wasn't going to have an abortion. No one was going to take my baby from me this time. Not ever.

FIGHTING for my daughter began at conception. I fought to keep her; I refused all who suggested that I abort her. I stood up for her and me, and eventually, everyone came around, even her father. My pregnancy was not an easy one.

Early in my pregnancy, my mom begged me to come back home to Florida. I just couldn't do it.

"Jill, come home. You can live with your dad and me, and we can help raise this baby as far away from Scott as possible." Her tone had changed from nine years earlier when she wanted nothing to do with a baby in her house. My heart still housed resentment toward her for that troubled time.

"I'm not coming home, Mom," I said with conviction. "I love Scott, and this is a chance for me to have a real family."

"You have a real family, Jill. You have us; you have Alex. And he misses his mommy so much."

There it was, the guilt trigger: my two-and-a-half-year-old son, Alex, the one I'd temporarily left with his father so that I could make a better life for all of us in Illinois. I planned to move to Illinois with Scott, land a good job, a decent apartment, get my baby boy, and live happily ever after. Things didn't happen the way I had planned. My fantasy was not working out the way I had dreamed of. Everyone warned me. They were right.

Depression took hold of me. I was lonely. I couldn't keep a job. Scott and I fought all the time. I lied to everyone about money, work, everything. I tried to convince myself, and everyone else that I had this great life and things were going just as planned. I created this alternative world that didn't exist. I was consumed with guilt for leaving my son in Florida and moving to Illinois. Once again, I ran away from everything, including my son. That's all I knew how to do. Runaway.

Although my pregnancy wasn't planned, it was the one thing that kept me going. I was fortunate that the Illinois Medicaid system and the team of assigned doctors were more along the lines of private health care than the public healthcare system offered in my home state of Florida. Once I applied and was accepted into the maternity program, I was seen at the Maclean County Health Department, given a complete exam, and assigned to my OBGYN, Dr. Jeffrey Galvin. I had no idea what to expect. The concept of "public aid" had always been a dirty word in our home, and according to my father, "only lazy losers" applied for help—the quintessential conservative mindset that I grew up with. My father's words kept ringing in my ears; my emotions started toying with me.

Am I a lazy loser? Is this how my father sees me? I am a disappointment to every man in my life, my father, my son, and my partner.

These thoughts predicated my future, and for years to come, stopped me dead in my tracks.

≈

WALKING into Dr. Galvan's office was a pleasant surprise. The office was in a newer building and beautifully decorated with modern art on the pastel-colored walls. When I arrived for my three-month check-up, the waiting room was quiet. It didn't even smell like a doctor's office—there was a scent of renewal. I'm not sure how to explain it or if there's even a discernible odor to "renewal," but whatever I smelled, that's what it felt like. There were a few other women with protruding, pregnant bellies, although mine was still a tiny bump. Unaccompanied, I gently shut the door behind me and flashed a half-crooked smile to the women who looked up. *What a beautiful waiting room*, I thought to myself; *these women sure don't look like losers to me; they look like SHEros, magnificent, expecting humans awaiting the arrival of their most precious gift.* My dad was wrong. Inside of that moment, inside of that building, I found myself feeling like I mattered. My baby and I mattered. And so did the other women. We are mothers doing the best we can—caring for ourselves and our babies.

The receptionist greeted me. Sliding the glass window that separated her desk from the waiting room, she smiled warmly, "Good morning, what's your name, please?"

"Jill Wilson," I said, feeling nervous. "I have an appointment at 9:30 a.m."

"Okay, first time here?"

"Yes, ma'am," trying to keep my voice from cracking.

"Thanks. Fill out this paperwork, and we'll call you back in just a few minutes. Who's your insurance through?" Shit. I knew she was going to ask that question.

"Um, it's, um, Medicaid," I felt ashamed to say the word, Me-di-caid.

"Okay, well, fill out this form instead—we accept many types of insurance in our office."

What? You mean, this place isn't for 'lazy losers?' My dad had it all wrong. I'd learn much later that my dad had a lot of things wrong about life and humanity.

It wasn't long before they called me back to the exam room to meet Dr. Galvan. He was young, tall, and very welcoming. His demeanor and voice were calming; I felt safe. We talked about my pregnancy and both of our expectations. It was very comforting. I left his office on top of the world. I went home and was excited to tell Scott all about my OBGYN visit. When he arrived home from class, I was in the kitchen sitting at our small kitchen table on one of the hunter-green resin chairs. He walked into the kitchen, and I couldn't contain my excitement. I so badly wanted to share all my pregnancy moments with him. "I met my doctor today," I said.

"Yeah?" he replied as he searched through the scarcely stocked refrigerator.

"Yes! You should see the office. It's nothing like I thought it was going to be like. It's so nice. The entire staff is helpful and caring, and Dr. Galvan is so wonderful. I'm so thankful he is my doctor. He measured my belly…."

"Wait, 'he'?" Scott stopped and looked at me with a confused look on his face.

"Yes, Dr. Galvan. He's incredible, and I feel really good about him delivering the baby.

"Really? A man? A man is going to look at your pussy? Hell, no."

"What do you mean, 'hell, no'? He's a doctor, and the doctor assigned to me through the insurance that I have to be on because you can't provide any for the baby or me."

"Fuck you, Jill."

"What the hell is your problem, Scott?"

He walked over to my chair, took his hand, and pulled the chair backward until I fell to the floor and landed on my back.

"Fuck you," he screamed at me. "I told you I wanted you to have a female doctor."

"Scott, I don't have a choice of doctors, okay? There's nothing wrong with this doctor."

"The hell there isn't. I don't want another guy in between your legs staring at your pussy...."

I was scared and crying. This is the second fall I had taken since I got pregnant. The first was a few weeks prior when I fell on the ice during the heart of winter (something this Florida girl was not prepared for). "What the hell did you do that for?" I hysterically yelled as I lay on my back in a sitting position with the chair still under me.

"You will not have a male gynecologist," he demanded. And in a second, he turned on his heel, walked toward the bedroom, and slammed the door.

I kept Dr. Galvan as my doctor. But through the years, the resentment toward Scott and his patriarchal, alpha-male demands pushed this young woman farther and farther away.

"JILL, your daughter needs to be born. We're afraid there's a problem with your umbilical cord—it isn't providing any nutrition to the baby. She's stopped growing. She's small, but we will induce your labor tomorrow if her lungs are developed enough. She has a better chance of survival on the outside so that we can monitor her eating. As of now, she's starving to death," my OBGYN said.

"Okay." I was worried, what if she starved to death tonight—can't we induce my labor now? I was petrified and wanted her out now. "How will we know if her lungs are developed?" I asked.

"We are going to do a stress test on you and the baby as well as an ultrasound," the doctor replied.

"What if her lungs aren't strong enough?"

"Let's take one thing at a time," he said with a deep sigh

pushing his Harry Potter glasses (and this was way before Harry Potter) up the bridge of his long, skinny nose. "Wait here, Ms. Wilson, I'll get the nurse, and she'll escort you to the testing room."

I was alone; Scott had class and couldn't take me to my weekly doctor's appointment—nothing out of the ordinary. As I waited in the cold exam room, I looked around, and a rush of memories began to flood my mind. I remembered when I was a little girl, and my mom would take me to the doctor. We would laugh so hard over nothing—we'd make funny outfits out of the paper gowns, and I'd read magazine articles impersonating different accents—we'd laugh until we cried. I had my mom all to myself.

I didn't have a lot of memories from my childhood when I felt safe, but when I was alone with my mom, that's when I felt her love in my center—a stark contrast to what I was feeling at that moment. The sterile, antiseptic smell, the posters of women's fallopian tubes, the dioramas of birthing vaginas were closing in on me. I could barely breathe. I was scared. What if my baby didn't make it? Was God punishing me for having an abortion as a teenager?

The door opened swiftly; the nurse immediately summoned me to the ultrasound room.

"Okay, Ms. Wilson. You're familiar with this procedure. Let's take a look at your baby girl." She smiled peacefully, and my loneliness drifted away for the time being. She squeezed the cold gel on my hard belly. I felt the baby kick as she firmly placed the sonogram wand on my lower abdomen. The nurse steadied the wand so we could hear the baby's heartbeat. Soon we heard a fast *thump, thump, thump, thump*—at about 120 beats per minute. Her heart sounded strong, and her lungs appeared to be developed enough for her to survive. I was scheduled for induction at 6 a.m. the following day.

~

CELIA WAS A VERY SICK BABY. She was born prematurely, and although her lungs were developed, her stomach was not, and she did not have the sucking instinct. She was admitted to the NICU for close observation. These two obstacles made feeding my baby problematic. I wasn't able to breastfeed because of her inability to suck. It was an extremely worrisome time for her father and me, but it did bring us closer than we had ever been. We didn't want to lose our baby girl, and we didn't know how to help her. Celia stayed in the hospital for about a week after she was born. I was fortunate because they allowed me to stay in a private room on the same floor as NICU to be with her all day and night.

There were many tests and x-rays that rough week, but finally she started eating independently and having bowel movements, which were all good signs. "It's time to take your baby home," the pediatrician told us one morning. We were elated and packed up to leave as soon as we signed the papers. During my pregnancy, we moved three times, the last being to Scott's mom's comfortable, finished basement just days before her birth. Anne had finally come to accept that we were having a baby, and knowing Celia would be born premature, she offered to help. And I'm glad she did.

Because of her underdeveloped stomach, she was prone to painful stomach issues. Celia had severe colic as a newborn. If you have ever experienced a colicky baby, my heart goes out to you. It is undeniably one of the most challenging times in the infancy stage; it will send you to the end of your threshold of patience. Don't ever be ashamed of asking for help if your baby suffers from colic. After caring for a colicky baby, you will never be the same again. Even all these years after her infancy, I can still hear, on replay, the continuous shrill and painful screams that emerged from her tiny, four-pound premie body. She would scream for hours on end. So much so that Scott, Anne, and I each took shifts. She would typically start screaming around 6 p.m. and usually end around 9 p.m. It was like clockwork for what seemed like years, but in reality, it was only the first three months of her life—my poor baby. We tried everything to help her. Eventually, she just grew out of it.

SCOTT and I married soon after Celia was born. Our relationship, however, was destined for destruction from the beginning. We never got along, not when we dated, and sure as hell not when we married. The truth is, we should have never been husband and wife. Our daughter would have been better off raised by the two of us separately, not together. What she witnessed as a child has long haunted her as an adult, and her dad and I are to blame for this mess.

By the time Celia turned eight, Scott and I were divorced. A nasty divorce left chunks of damage control in reestablishing and building a solid mother/daughter relationship that her father tried his damnedest to destroy. However, I caused just as much damage between my daughter and me with the choices I made in my life.

I cheated on Scott several times and with more than one man. I'm not proud of my actions, and if I had to do it all over again, I would have never committed adultery—not out of respect for him, an abuser doesn't deserve respect, but out of respect for the vows I made to God and as a role model for my daughter. My daughter was too young to understand what was going on. Still, it would not have allowed Scott to plant negative ideas, thoughts, and language into Celia's foundation-forming mind. It turned out to be detrimental for years to come and well into her adulthood.

~

SCOTT and I divorced in 2003; it was ugly and painful. For about a year after the divorce, we tried a few times to reconcile using sex as a tool to heal the relationship. The sex healed nothing; it complicated everything. We permanently cut ties in mid-2004.

CHAPTER 7

The mother-daughter bond may give rise to the deepest mutuality and the most painful estrangement. It is an intense yet uneasy affinity braided out of the many conflicting emotions, guilt, love, recognition, hatred, rage.
~Rita Felski

*S*ince her childhood, specifically, when her father and I started divorce proceedings, my relationship with Celia has been like sliding across black ice. For years, I made grave mistakes in my personal life, which largely impacted the adult relationship with my daughter. As of today, it's non-existent.

There's been nothing in my life more devastating than that of the strained and threadbare relationship with my Celia. At the penning of this book, we haven't spoken in over a year; I haven't laid my eyes on her in six years. I voyeuristically try and follow her on social media sites—anything for a glimpse into her life to know how she is doing and that she's okay, but all I see is the shrapnel she's left behind; she's blocked me or set her pages to private. She wants nothing to do with me.

I accept the responsibility for the severed relationship. However, I did not choose to walk away. Celia chose the path and is unrelenting, unforgiving, and unaccepting of my apologies or willingness to work on things together. Every day, I'm saddled with the guilt and shame of not being the mother that I should have been or the role model I desperately wanted to be. However, I'm saddened by my daughter's lack of empathy and inability to consider any idea of reconciliation. Perhaps she's internally forgiven my shortcomings; I can't speak to that. If she has, hopefully, it has brought peace to her life. I acknowledge that my lack of mothering wholly affected my daughter and destroyed our future as mother and daughter, a vital bond. Yes, I can blame her father for myriad issues that contributed to the brokenness, but I am ultimately responsible for my part in this. One thing I am sure of is the weight of a person's upbringing profoundly affects their ability to function as an adult.

When I think of reparation and forgiveness through the lens of dysfunction, I can't say I blame her for wanting nothing to do with me.

UNTIL RECENTLY, I carried within me the heart of that little seven-year-old girl listening to her parents' conversation about how deeply her big brother resented her existence or how she was the "midlife mistake" or what a burden she was on her mother because she didn't behave or walk or talk or act exactly the way her mother wanted.

I see how these conversations shaped my entire life and the half of a "whole" person I grew into. I never felt like I belonged anywhere, and more than anything, I wanted to belong, especially to a man, because that's what my mother told me "mattered the most." From a very young age, my mother made it clear that a woman finds her value through a man's love and acceptance: the 1950s housewife and cult of domesticity mindset. I started dreaming of the perfect man, wedding, and children at a very young age. It was an escape from the mental and physical abuse I endured growing up. I was a child trying to morph into a woman far too young and without my parents' guidance or direction. I had no identity of my own. I believed my identity would be formed in the arms and bed of a man, someone who could take care of me. I believed my body—the aesthetic—was the only tool I needed to feel worthy of love. It took many years, many partners, and a lot of bad, unwanted sex to break that mindset.

Not only were there a myriad of intimate relationships in my life, but I mirrored my mother's behavior with my daughter as I raised her. My mother was a screamer. Granted, I was not always the most well-behaved kid, but my mother screamed or cried or threatened me as a child whenever things didn't go the way she was hellbent on making them go. That's how I treated my daughter—verbatim (both of my kids, actually). These patterns trickled deep into the caverns of my behavior; its effects were inimical. I imitated what I saw growing up—what was modeled as the "way to parent." I never physically abused my children, but I also didn't protect them from my "learned" parenting techniques.

My daughter's middle school years were tough on us, especially on her. I went from one dysfunctional relationship to the next. As my world was crashing down on me, I allowed my drama to seep into her life. I created a very unstable environment for her, yet I tried to hold on to her with a vice grip. Even at the young age of eleven, she knew that our environment wasn't healthy. And the only way Celia knew how to tell me was to try her hardest to get away from me, which she did pretty frequently.

I didn't mother her the way she deserved and yearned to be mothered. She was way more intelligent than I gave her credit for; kids usually are. I went from long-term relationship to short-term relationship, a third short-lived marriage, and an unhealthy eighteen-month relationship with a man I refer to as Fifty Shades of Shit.

I moved my daughter and me from house to house, and, frankly, she grew weary and untrusting of my ability to discern between a good decision and a bad one. Celia grew tired of the fights between me and whoever I was dating or married to. She grew tired of having to wipe away my tears after the last break-up. She grew tired of new people coming in and out of her life— our life. Conversely, her father had a stable life. He had been in a stable relationship and marriage with the same woman since we'd divorced and that felt safe to Celia.

In the moment and through my own chaos, I didn't listen to her clarion cry for my attention. I was too busy trying to mother myself as a grown woman without the slightest clue what I was doing to my little girl.

I often say that if I could have one mulligan it would be motherhood. Now that my daughter is a grown woman, I look in the rearview mirror of her childhood with much angst. I am hard on myself. I could have, I should have, done a better job. To this day, I look at other mothers and internally scold myself: *why couldn't I have been like that mother?* Without even knowing their personal story, I automatically award other mothers a medal of honor while compartmentalizing myself into the "bad mom's club," where I am the sole member and forever-president.

Sometimes, when I see mothers and daughters out shopping, eating, laughing, loving, I begin shape-shifting, morphing the faces of the duos into the faces of Celia and me—stepping out of my world and into that relationship—fiercely wishing, pretending that it's us. Time stops: for a brief flash, my heart is whole as I fulfill the moments I'm no longer privileged to share with her. The moments, present and future, that I no longer get to call ours. Reality is crushing. I blink, and the faces of these strangers become the most authentic rendering of our relationship—unidentifiable. I begin beating myself up until once again, my emotions coil into the fetal position dying a death I wouldn't wish on any mother, ever. I crawl into a corner of myself—a space no one can get to.

If I'm feeling this way, how must she have felt? Perhaps this is how she felt when I didn't bother to hear her begging for my singular attention, "Mommy, can't it be just the two of us? Why do you need a boyfriend? Why do you need a husband?"

"Celia, baby, I deserve to be loved, too," I'd say. *But isn't my love enough, Mommy?* That's what she was trying with all her might to tell me.

Mother's Day is the worst day of the year. With my mother deceased and the estranged relationship with my daughter, Mother's Day is solemn and heavy. I don't want to get out of bed, I can't look at social media, talk to my friends, and I don't want to celebrate mothers. I know this is selfish. Every Mother's Day, I'm swallowed whole by the quicksand of shame—it engulfs me in seconds. It squeezes the very breath out of my soul and leaves me for dead. There are no more phone calls, cards, or Mother's Day brunches with the two women whose bodies I was once connected to. The cord is cut. The only thing tying us together are the memories. And that's what Mother's Day has become—a memory. An assortment of thoughts that break me. I can't get out of my own head.

I open my nightstand to the right of my bed. I reach for the leatherbound Bible that holds the cards of many past Mother's Days. The one on top is the last card I received from my Celia: Mother's Day 2013. I trace my polished index finger over the words she lovingly wrote:

Happy Mother's Day Mama. Thank you for all you do for me and

all the love and support you give—only you could do it. I love you! Love,
Celia. Xoxo

The grudge my daughter holds against me is heavy, and I can't carry it anymore. As hard as it is to move on, I still have to live even if most days I feel like I can't breathe.

CHAPTER 8

The bitterest tears shed over graves are for words left unsaid and
deeds left undone.

~Harriet Beecher Stowe

LARRY

*A*ugust 31, 1997. The media coverage of Princess Diana's
fatal Paris car crash had been on television for hours. I
was beginning to doze off as the early morning sun woke after a
night of watching the world learn we'd lost our Princess. My
two-year-old daughter was snuggled next to me, sleeping
soundly, when the phone rang. I reached for the cordless handset
sitting on the tattered, hand-me-down end table, next to the pull-
out couch that doubled as our bed. The caller ID read "James
Wilson." It was my parents' shared cell phone. I figured Mom was
calling about the news of Princess Diana. Dazed and half asleep, I
answered, my voice sounding like a dusty old record: "Hello?"

"Jill? There's an emergency." My mother sounded panicked. I thought something had happened to my father, who for twenty years had suffered from emphysema and whose health was progressively deteriorating. A few days ago, I'd spoken to her and knew they were at St. Petersburg Beach for the week, so her call was a surprise.

"What happened? Is Dad okay?"

"Dad is fine. It's Larry," she said.

She tried to stay composed as she told me that my oldest brother, who was forty-eight, had suffered a thoracic aortic aneurysm.

"We are leaving the beach and headed to south Florida right now," she explained.

Groggy and confused, I tried to sort through her words. I didn't know what a thoracic aortic aneurysm was. "What does this mean, Mom? Is he dead?"

"No, but he is in a coma in critical condition and in trauma ICU at Delray Medical Center. They don't think he's going to make it. You need to come home and say your goodbyes." I could feel her pain radiate through the phone; my heart began pounding loud and fast, making it difficult to process all my mother was trying to tell me. My brother, twenty years my elder, was dying.

I lived in Bloomington, Illinois, with my husband, Scott, and youngest daughter, Celia. My five-year-old son was living with his father in Maryland. Scott was finishing his bachelor's degree at Illinois State University, I had a small home daycare business, and cocktail waitressed at night. I was twenty-eight, in an unhappy and abusive second marriage.

My mother explained that Larry had been experiencing excruciating back pain the evening before and drove himself to the ER. Tests indicated that an aortic aneurysm was en route from his back, and once it reached his brain, he would be dead. Without immediate surgery, he would die in a matter of days.

The diagnosis: a 20 percent chance of surviving surgery; they would try and intercept the blood clot and remove it.

∼

GROWING UP, both of my brothers were active in sports. Larry and Kenny played on the same high school football team, although Larry's talents shined brighter than Kenny's. By his senior year of high school, Larry was offered a scholarship to play football at every top ten Division I college in the nation. This was a big deal not only for our family but for the community. He signed with the University of Miami, our family's alma mater. The media made a production of their hometown sports hero Larry Wilson—the family celebrity.

Larry and I were never close, but he was my brother, and throughout my life, he was a person I longed for acceptance from. How I wished the feelings were reciprocated. My brother didn't approve of anything I did and made that clear to my parents and other family members. Larry had been bitter over my existence since my parents told him they were pregnant. The story of his reaction he proudly retold to a large audience of family members during my father's surprise fiftieth birthday celebration. I was ten years old at the time and in attendance.

Larry stood at the makeshift podium with his speech in hand, where he was the milestone event's master of ceremony. As Larry unpacked the history of our father, more in line with a midlife "roast," he recounted the day he found out my mother was pregnant with me.

"I was so mad at them," he remembered with a passive chuckle, shifting from one leg to the other leaning on one arm, "I looked at my forty-year-old parents and asked them, 'how could you do this? How could you let this happen? What am I going to tell my friends? They're going to know what the two of you have been doing. Shouldn't you be preparing for grandchildren instead of decorating a nursery?"

The warm, fall Florida air turned chilly as I sat between my parents, arms folded in my lap, watching and listening to my brother tell the fifty-plus guests that he disapproved of them having another baby. Making it clear he was not happy about my parents' carelessness, he wanted everyone to know, including me. Larry never allowed us to be close; he only knew the Jill he constructed, not the one who longed for a relationship with her big brother.

Larry's football accomplishments segued into business success and philanthropic endeavors. In the high-end South Florida communities of Boca Raton and West Palm Beach, my brother quickly rose to success as a prominent general contractor and multimillion-dollar supporter of promising young athletes and collegiate athletic programs. Everyone loved Larry, his generous donations, and his larger-than-life personality. It seemed like I was the only one not allowed to get too close to the self-made celebrity. If "influencer" had been a thing in the 1990s, Larry would have certainly played the role to perfection.

DESPITE A LIFETIME OF DIFFERENCES, I wanted to see my brother. Within twenty-four hours, I was on a plane to South Florida. Over the next few days, family members arrived at the hospital and were in and out of Larry's room for short visits. My sister Cindy and other brother Kenny were there; Larry's grown children, nieces, nephews, friends, and extended family members made their way to see the man everyone adored. Larry was in and out of consciousness; recovery looked bleak.

The hospital waiting room was home for the week I was there; friends would take turns bringing food in for the family.

We wanted to stay close in case his condition changed for the better or worse. We were all holding out for hope.

Finally, it was my turn to see my brother. After the troubled relationship we shared, I was nervous. I didn't know what I would say to this man I loved but who seemed to hate me for being born. I didn't want to upset him.

My mom looked at me. "You can go now, Jill."

"Are you sure this is a good idea?" I asked.

"Yes, I told him you were here. He can't talk with the ventilator, but he squeezed my hand," she said. "Go on. Tell him you love him. That's all you need to say. He will hear you."

I walked into the sterile Intensive Care Unit. The nurse directed me to his room.

There he was, completely helpless. I'd never seen Larry vulnerable before. He was always so strong, sure of himself, intimidating (at least to me, he was). The room was cold; the jarring sounds of the ventilator were startling. The humanlike machine was breathing 100 percent for Larry. First a beep, then a gush of air forced into his lungs. He was lying flat on his back, his eyes closed. Broken. His left leg had been amputated earlier that week after gangrene set in. The starch-white hospital sheet fell flat at the bend where his calf should have met the knee, indicating there was no more leg left to cover.

I looked to the side of his bed to get a glimpse at the long white tube stretched from the man-made lungs keeping him alive. It was secured by a clear plastic strap attached to one side of his mouth, pulled around his neck, and attached to the opposite side. Above the machine, his vitals were displayed. A rhythmic beat... his heart was in a steady rhythm. Everything seemed stable, but the machines supported him. Without the support, he would die. Even Larry needed help.

I walked over to the side of his bed, bent down close to his head, and whispered, "Hi Larry, it's your sister Jill." He heard me, and although his eyes were closed, he tried to move his arms. "I wanted to come to see you." I took his hand and held it. "I want you to know that I love you."

He squeezed my hand and tried opening his eyes. This was a moment that was all ours. Brother and sister, twenty years apart, but at that moment, we couldn't have been closer. I sat there in the stillness, taking it all in. I was allowed to love him. No one could take that moment or that memory away from me. This is the closest we'd been in my lifetime. The ventilator silenced him, but the squeeze of his hand spoke louder than any conversation we'd ever had.

Twenty days later, after the fight of his life, Larry passed away due to complications from a thoracic aortic aneurysm. Larry's death was the first of four significant losses over the next twelve years.

~

KENNY

On September 11, 2001, an unprecedented war was waged on America. However, a few months prior, what felt like war, was waged on our family. My beloved brother Kenny succumbed to a long battle of mental and physical illness at fifty. By the end of June 2001, my parents laid two sons to rest, and my sister and I lost two brothers. It felt so unfair.

Kenny was nineteen years older than me, but we were the closest of my three siblings. We shared a connection that I didn't feel with my other brother or sister. Kenny was always the underdog, the son that lived in the shadows, and the son that didn't quite measure up to our older brother's talent and our father's expectations.

Although Kenny was a talented quarterback, he was over-looked by the "big" schools like Larry. He had a short stint playing football for a small college in North Carolina but quit after a few semesters. Not long after arriving home, Kenny announced, "I'm going to Vietnam."

He trained to be an MP (military police) and was deployed to Okinawa. A few years later, by the time I was three, he was home from the war and planning to marry a girl named Jill from New Jersey. Jill was the best friend of Larry's new wife. We now had two Jill Wilsons in the family.

From then on, I was referred to as "Little Jill." That name stuck with me for a very long time.

My brother Kenny was tethered to a dark past from as far back as I can remember. Alcohol was his vice. Often he would disappear, running from the deep inner turmoil and demons that chased him. He'd go on drinking binges and not tell anyone where he was for long periods, sometimes years. Then, out of the blue, he'd call to say he was drunk and living on the streets and needed someone to pick him up and take him to a halfway house. Or he'd come home clean and sober with a good job, married to some new woman, or living with a new flame. This happened for the first thirty years of my life.

This was the only Kenny I knew. Cindy and Larry knew Kenny before the war, before the pain buried itself in the crevices of his core, before he could understand the weight of his demons, and before the pressure of life took him out. Just like me, Kenny was a runner, too. He just ran a little farther and harder than I did. We were the two out of four children that disappointed our parents the most. And they didn't have a problem letting us know this.

KENNY WAS EXTREMELY handsome and very charming. His sense of humor won over friends and family—he had nine lives and lived every one of them to their fullest. For Kenny, it was all or nothing. There was no middle ground for him. He was either binging or clean. When he was binging, he was out of control. When he was sober, he had the world by the balls and could do anything he put his mind to. He was also manic-depressive but without an official diagnosis, understanding, or acceptance from our family.

He left his wife and children several times over many years. He staged his own kidnapping and, years later, staged his own death. A few years before he died, he went missing. His brand-new SUV was found on a bridge somewhere in Louisiana. The authorities feared Kenny had jumped to his death. I was devastated the day I received the call from my mother.

"How will we know for sure?" I asked.

"We won't unless someone finds his body," she said.

I'd only heard her voice sound so deflated and hopeless one other time: when she called to tell me about Larry. She said they would not look for his body; someone would have to report finding it. The authorities told her he left his car keys in the ignition and his wallet in the passenger seat. They also said this was a bridge where many suicides had been reported. There would be no closure for anyone unless his body was found.

And no one was even going to look for him.

"Have you told Dad yet?" I asked.

Kenny had disappeared so many times in his life my father wanted nothing to do with him and boldly stated that he disowned him after the last episode.

"Yes, he said he doesn't care."

"Mom, you know that's not true; he cares. He's just too stubborn to admit it or to show any emotion. We all know that Dad cares," I said.

"I'm not so sure of that. His heart has turned to stone when it comes to your brother," she said.

If anyone knew my dad could be cold toward his children, it was me. He hated my daughter's father so much that he vowed not to pay a dime toward our wedding, walk me down the aisle, or even attend. Yet, he showed up. He surprised me. He walked me down the aisle and paid for the open bar at our reception.

Why did our father have to pretend to have a cold heart? Couldn't he see that we were begging for his love?

ONE AFTERNOON, a few years later, I was cleaning my tiny apartment when the house phone rang. I didn't recognize the number on the caller ID.

"Hello?" I heard a familiar voice on the other end.

"Jillzie!" A male's voice exclaimed. It was my brother, Kenny.

"Kenny? Is this you?" Tears filled my eyes, and a lump of love choked back my words.

"Hey, sis. It's me," he said. I paused for a minute. Closing my eyes, wishing I could conference in my mom. "Kenny, where the hell have you been? We thought you were dead. Have you called Mom?" I had so many questions that demanded answers immediately but didn't want to risk him hanging up on me.

"No, I haven't called Mom," he replied.

"She needs to know you're alive." I was crying and trying to catch my breath.

"I know, I'll call her. I love you, sis. I'll see you soon."

Dial tone.

My brother was alive. I reset the phone and called my mom. I could barely contain myself. "Mom," I said, "Kenny just called me. He's alive."

"What do you mean, you just talked to him? He's alive?"

EVENTUALLY, Kenny made it back home and got sober (again). His two years away were rough; he damaged his body by smoking and drinking himself to near death. He was no longer able to work or do much of anything. He was just shy of fifty. The relationship between my brother and father was superficial. Dad tolerated Kenny, but I don't think he ever forgave him for his past mistakes: or more so, for not being Larry. By the time my brother was back home, Scott and I had moved from Illinois back to Brandon. We lived in a condo that my parents generously purchased and we paid the mortgage. Kenny was getting sicker and more depressed. Like my father, he had chronic obstructive pulmonary disease, and his lungs could not function at much capacity.

Kenny lived alone and on disability in a small apartment in Dunedin, Florida, where the walls were closing in on him. His mind would play tricks on him, and the depression haunted his every move. He would often call me late at night and want to tell me jokes or complain about something he saw in the news. When he did, he was always drunk. In his stupor, he began drinking and, unbeknownst to us, smoking again. In early June 2001, my mother called to tell me that Kenny had been admitted to the Veteran's Hospital in St. Petersburg, Florida. He called 911 from his apartment.

Kenny had fallen out of his wheelchair onto the floor by the time the first responders arrived. There were ashtrays and vodka bottles strewn throughout the apartment. His lungs had collapsed.

After a month of hospitalization, a chest tube to help him breathe, and a lack of oxygen to the brain he lost his ability to decipher fantasy from reality. My brother was hallucinating and reliving his days in the Vietnam War. He would call and tell me these wild stories about how someone was outside his window trying to kill him.

"I'm being held against my will, and someone needs to rescue me." He pleaded for me to take him home.

The hospital was about an hour from where I lived. My mother lived about a mile from me, so we had a long drive. She rarely went to see him. She told me it was just too painful. I tried to go at least two times a week. Even if he were sleeping, I would talk to him and tell him I was there. He was in full force other times telling me all kinds of crazy war stories. Except they weren't a memory, they were his reality. He lived in a war zone every day, both mentally and physically.

The call came a few weeks later. My mother called to tell me that Kenny was on a ventilator. He pulled his chest tube out, trying to escape his "war captors." He was hallucinating, and no one in the hospital would help him. He tried to call the nurses' station and tell them there were "men with big guns" outside his window, and he was scared. No one would pay attention to my big brother, not the nurses, not the doctors. He was afraid, and he wanted to run like he always did. This time would be the last.

Kenny was pronounced brain dead. As the family gathered by his side, the mood was somber. The room was a cocktail of sadness and death. Like Larry, there were tubes, beeps, and blankets to keep him warm. Although the walls were stark white, the air was gray. My God. How could I be losing another brother? How would my parents ever overcome this tragedy? I looked over at my father, who was then in a wheelchair, and my mother, as they watched another son leave the earth. The doctor arrived a few minutes later after speaking with Kenny's grown children about options.

"Mr. and Mrs. Wilson, as you know, your son is brain dead. These machines keep him alive, but nothing is happening in his brain. He does not have a 'DNR' on file, so we cannot turn off his life support legally until a team of doctors deems your son is clinically brain dead. At this time, I have the signature of five hospital doctors. His children have elected to have his ventilator removed." The doctor looked down at his chart and scribbled something.

I looked over at my parents, and my father, who was at my brother's bedside, he looked beyond his son and out the window into the dark world. Although it was night, I'm positive the world would have appeared dim at any time of the day. My father sat emotionless, clearing his throat. My mom looked at her son and placed her hand on his. Both of her boys, gone.

The doctor looked up from his chart, "The nurse will be in shortly to remove his ventilator, tubes, and all medicine. He should pass quickly. Pneumonia has settled in his lungs and he has no reflexes left. He will not be able to breathe on his own once the breathing tube is out."

We said our goodbyes as the nurse arrived. I wanted to give my mom and dad some time alone with Kenny, so I left the room. I asked the nurse if she could wait a minute or two and let our parents say their goodbyes privately. My father broke his gaze from the vastness of the dark, "I don't need any more time. Johnnie, I'll be in the hall." I was shocked that he wouldn't support my mother and say goodbye to his son.

"I'll be out in a minute," she said. The nurse stood toward the back of the small room and gave my mom the time she needed. I don't know what my mother said to her dying son in those last moments, but I know he heard it. In a few minutes, my mother met us in the hall. She looked at my dad and said, "Let's go, Jim. I can't do this again. I can't watch another child of mine die before my eyes." And before I could respond, she looked at me, "I'm sorry, Jill. Do you have a ride home?"

"Yes, ma'am. But don't you want to stay for a while?"

"No," she said sharply. And left.

I stayed and watched my brother slowly fade from this earthly life into eternal life with his Heavenly Father, where he would no longer suffer. He fought until the bitter end.

"Goodbye, Kenny. I love you." It was all I had left to say. I took the memories of my brother and housed them in a sacred place. I revisit them frequently.

~

IN FOUR YEARS, my parents laid two sons to rest, and by March 2004, I lost my father. I lost more than half of my immediate family inside of seven years.

In 2003, two years after Kenny died, my mother suffered a heart attack, stroke and underwent a quadruple bypass. She survived but was faced with months of recovery, physical therapy, a diagnosis of congestive heart failure, and damage to her eyesight due to the stroke. My father was in the final stages of emphysema and getting worse by the day. They both needed care. During this time, my husband, Scott, filed for divorce and left me with no car, no money, and a custody fight for my daughter that I could not afford. I felt helpless, and Scott was making everything worse by threatening to take my daughter from me permanently. As my divorce and nasty custody battle ensued, I was forced to move back in with my parents. Again. I hadn't lived with them for years, and although our relationship had been somewhere between love and resentment, during that time, we were all using each other for exactly what we needed from the other—codependency with a heaping side of brewed resentment.

By January of 2004, my father's health took a turn for the worse, and in March, he lost his twenty-four-year battle with emphysema. My mother was single for the first time in 56 years.

Mom

My relationship with my mother underwent many iterations over the five years between Dad's death and her passing. In the months following my father's death, my mom had been in and out of the hospital due to the complications of congestive heart failure. A few years later, my mother and I decided to move in together. I would be able to keep an eye on her making sure she got to all her doctor appointments and overseeing her medications. She sold the home she shared with my father for over thirty years, and we became roommates.

Admittedly, I was not the best roommate (or daughter) for many reasons; in hindsight, our relationship would have fared much better had we not decided to share our living arrangements. Once we lived together as two adult women, the wall of shame and resentment of my past began closing in on me. Everything about my mother got under my skin. The memories of my childhood and teenage years haunted me at a subconscious level. Although the memories had always been there, it was different because I was older and able to stand outside the pain. It always sucked me back in and was fresh in my mind and heart. I never forgot how she made me feel when I was a teenage girl, especially, the abortion. I harbored that anger for years; it was like traveling back in time when I looked at her. It dumped me right in the center of each moment. Resentment toward my mother was at a fever pitch.

After living together for a few years, we had a terrible parting of ways. I was triggered by something she said during a heavy and hurtful conversation; the pain and oppression of my adolescence came crashing down like an angry avalanche of thick, heavy mountain rock. Once I started on her, I didn't stop until she grabbed her purse, keys, and phone. Her health left her in no condition to be driving, but I did a fantastic job of driving her out.

She'd had enough, made a call, and sat in her car waiting for a family member to pick her up and take her somewhere far away from me, the truth, the lies, the pain, everything I was throwing at her: everything she was absorbing, denying, and abandoning, all at once, in her most vulnerable moments.

Regardless of my inner pain and dire need to shred that layer of my life, it was the wrong time and inappropriate manner to unload everything I had carried deep in my soul for thirty-nine years. It is a regret I will bear for the rest of my life. Conversely, the conversation needed to happen—my only wish is that the timing would have been different.

The last image of my mother etched in my memory is her helplessly sitting in her car as I stood at my front window fighting the urge to take her in my arms and apologize for hurting her even though she had hurt me. My pride overshadowed all common sense as I watched her go. It was the very last time I saw my mother's face. To this day, that very image continues to haunt me.

Within a few weeks, my mother made arrangements to move in with my sister, requiring her to move across the country to Arkansas, where my sister and her family (grown daughter and grandchildren) lived. Our fight had been so damaging; I had no desire to speak with her. She had been living with Cindy for only a few weeks when the call came telling me that she had taken a bad fall and fractured her hip.

"Mom will be having her hip replaced," my sister said.

"Isn't surgery dangerous at her age and with her damaged heart?" I asked.

"Well, that's what the doctor has suggested and the decision we have made."

Her response was matter-of-fact and curt. We hadn't been on good terms for years, and negative feelings were exacerbated in light of the rift between Mom and me. I was concerned but didn't feel I had the right or an invitation to discuss my feelings on medical matters involving our mother. Not long after the surgery, mom's health got progressively worse. It was the beginning of the end.

IN MY MOTHER'S HONOR, I decided to enroll in a GED course in the evenings at the local high school. We had to take a pretest to see where we needed the most help. I was so nervous, sure I'd fail, but determined to try. Before losing my mom, I wanted to take whatever preparatory classes I needed to pass the test. I wanted her to be proud of me. I longed to feel some redemption for the rift in our relationship. I went the following evening to receive my results. I noticed a diverse group of people: single mothers balancing their children between their hip and stroller; senior citizens showing themselves, and others, that it was never too late for an education; teenagers who had dropped out of school; and me. *Where do I fit in*, I asked myself? I had no identity, no sense of belonging, and no truth to lean on.

When it was finally my turn to see an adult night-school guidance counselor, I smiled and walked up to the man standing behind the long counter. He took the pencil between his teeth and tucked it behind his ear. He stoically looked at me, looked down, and asked my name. He shuffled through his papers as I listened to other counselors repeating the same question to prospective students.

"You did very well on these preliminary tests. You had a near-perfect score on the reading and writing portion. Math was a little low, but nothing a few prep classes can't help with; science and social studies, you did fine. Great job," he said.

Finally, a smile out of the guy. I was shocked and proud and couldn't wait to tell someone who knew the truth: that I had never graduated from high school.

After I registered for my math class, I was on top of the world. On my long and reflective walk to the car through the fluorescent-lit, stark white hall, I began making plans for my future. With a high school diploma, I could do anything, and the first thing I would do was enroll in college. I started picturing myself in the regalia I had never worn twenty-two years earlier when I dropped out of school. I fantasized about the future degree(s) I would hang on my wall and the feeling of accomplishment that I would have. I would also be a role model for my kids and other women. My mom would be proud of me.

As I was pulling out of the school parking lot and heading for home, my sister called to give me an update on our ailing mother. She had not been doing well and was going into hospice care. After we talked about Mom, I decided to share my good news. I thought she would be proud of me. "Well, Cindy, I did it. I've finally decided to get my GED," I said with a wide smile and a sigh of accomplishment.

"Okay," she said, sounding like I was offending her.

"I took the pretest, and I scored high on all the tests except math. So, all I have to do is take a few prep classes, and I should be ready for the actual test in a few weeks. I'm so excited. I hope Mom is proud of me. This is something she's wanted me to do for years."

"She won't even know what you are talking about, Jill. She's very disoriented." Cindy replied through a sarcastic, muffled laugh.

The lack of emotion hit like a baseball bat to the skull.

"I need to go. I'll keep you updated on mom. Bye." She hung up. I was deflated. I went to one math class and quit.

It wasn't just my sister's response that made me feel deflated but a compounding of my inner turmoil and shame. I didn't know how to save myself. And no one could do it for me.

It wasn't too many months after Mom had broken her hip and undergone surgery that her organs began to fail, and she was put into hospice care. My sister and I spoke several times a week as she would give me updates on Mom.

"Jill, mom isn't doing well. We've decided to turn off her pacemaker. It won't be long before she goes into complete organ failure," Cindy said.

My heart ached because I didn't have the money to travel from Florida to Arkansas to see her. And my sister held that grudge against me for years. Still, I needed to speak to my mother one more time, and Cindy was the gatekeeper.

"Is there a way I can speak with her? Is she able to talk to me over the phone?" I asked my sister.

"Maybe," she said. "Call her nurse a little later and see if she's alert enough to speak with you."

Stoic, bitter, empty answers.

I dialed the hospice line a few hours later and spoke with her nurse. She said Mom was awake and could talk. She handed the phone to my mother.

"Hello?" she said, sounding like herself.

"Hi, Mommy," I said.

"Jill, is this you? Why are you calling me? You were just here."

"No, Mom, I wasn't. I'm in Florida. I haven't talked to you in a while, and I just wanted to tell you I love you."

I could barely get the words out through the tears.

"Why are you crying, Jill?" she asked.

"I don't know, Mom. Your voice, I just don't ever want to forget your voice."

"Jill, I don't know why you are upset," she sounded annoyed with me. "You were just here. You were singing for Daddy and me, Larry and Kenny."

She was sure I had been there minutes before our call. I wasn't going to argue.

"I'm so glad you liked my singing, Mommy."

"Jill, you know I always love your singing. But I have to go now. Your dad is still here, and we're talking. The boys left, and it's just us. Come back tomorrow and sing for me, okay?"

"Okay, Mommy. I'll be back tomorrow."

"Bye, Jillzie. I love you."

"I love you, Mom." She hung up the phone.

That was the last time I spoke to my mother. She went home to the Lord and was reunited with her husband and sons a few days later.

There were so many things I didn't get to say.

PART II
THE COMEBACK

CHAPTER 9

*T*alk about your failures without apologizing.
~Brené Brown

IN THE YEARS following my mother's death, I was lost. Although our relationship was strained, facing my future without her was daunting and uncomfortable. There was an emptiness at the center of my existence that I couldn't grapple with. I was consistently in a liminal space of resentment and deep grief from losing the woman I'd always run to and eventually run from. I was forty years old and realized I didn't know how to do life without the toxic relationship I had with my mother. I continued entering into dysfunctional relationships because that was all I learned how to do. I was carelessly drawn to men whose love was wrapped in conditions or who just weren't emotionally available. Of course, I thought I could control every situation by charming each partner with my looks, sex, and manipulation. That's what I was taught to do, and that was how I identified my worth.

Alcohol, food, and men were my Band-Aids, my go-to feel

better, a way to numb the reality of my life that kept me in shackles, unable to uncover my truth. Day after day, I was a walking wreck, looking for someone I could fall into. I fell into some deep potholes during that time.

The summer before my mom died, I married for a third time, an old acquaintance from middle/high school. We dated for a year before she passed and married the summer prior. She knew him, liked him, and lived with us in his ramshackle place that could barely be considered a home. The marriage was a clusterfuck. It lasted eight miserable months and was another toxic mistake of mine. And another notch on my belt of stupid decisions that made up the majority of my life. I just kept wrapping that bitch of a belt around and around and around myself.

Although it was clear that the relationship would end, the marriage wasn't even over, and I began seriously dating someone else. Thank God we didn't get married. He was the midlife version of the character Christian Grey, a powerful and dominating millionaire who cared only about money, power, and womanizing.

After a year and a half, that yielded another failed attempt at a relationship. Nothing worked out for me because I didn't value or respect myself. Instead, I looked for my worth inside the minds of unhealthy relationships with men.

ENOUGH. My life had been spinning out of control for as long as I could remember, and I couldn't do it anymore. The red flags had been flying, and I ignored them my entire life. The thing with red flags is that we are often blind to them. Not colorblind, just blind. It's not something we do on purpose. It centers around our space, culture, community, and upbringing: our human conditions. As a child, I was taught about "red flags," but only those my parents wanted me to see: the ones most parents teach their children to recognize, the standard ones that typically have to do with not taking candy from strangers and avoiding rides in unfamiliar cars, not the ones that caution you from yourself. The space of chaos became my comfort zone until it reached its peak, like a boiling pot of water, spilling its contents, leaving third-degree burns on contact.

After the breakup with the fifty-shades-of-shit-middle-aged-Cristian Gray, I began to feel an internal shift of empowerment. For the first time in forty years, I didn't want or need a man in my life. I was tired of feeling powerless in my relationships, not only with men but across the board. My daughter was a junior in high school, and I finally felt an organic bond building between us. There was nothing that I allowed to take me away from being 100 percent present in her life.

I was staying home more and not going out with friends or men. I walked away from music for a while and started a new business. I was tired of being gone five to six nights a week and on weekends.

My daughter was tired of it, too; she never liked that I was a musician and would often ask, "Why can't you just be like other moms with normal jobs?"

I would explain that gigging was my job and put food on the table and a roof over our heads. She accepted it but never liked it. So, I decided to look for something else. After some research, I started a nanny/caregiver placement agency.

It felt like a rebirth. After many difficult years, there was a sense of wholeness between Celia and me. For the first time, no man took up space in my daughter's life. And, for the first time in my life, I was entirely in control of myself. The turning point came one night when I was home alone. Celia was at her dad's for the evening, and for the first time in a long time, I found myself sitting in the stillness, an utterly unrecognizable place. As the stillness reached out to me, I felt the tug to converse with God.

Growing up Lutheran, I was taught to pray. I prayed the proverbial prayers at the designated times: dinner, bedtime, and church on Sundays. But that moment was different. I was overtaken by emotion. In the shadows of my dimly lit bedroom at the foot of my bed, I fell to my knees, placed my hands on the ground, and cried out to the Lord, "God, You are here. I am not alone. I ask You to hear my cry. I've messed up so many times. I have no idea how to love or be loved. I can't find the truth in my life, and I'm broken. God, I'm broken."

The tears streamed down my face as the day's mascara stained the carpet below me. I surrendered, "It's yours, Lord. My pain is yours. My heart is yours. Guide me. I know I've let you down. I'm sorry, Lord. I've let my kids down. I've let myself down. Take it from me. Please help me to be the mother you intended me to be. If there is someone out there for me, I trust you will show me."

I sat with my knees tucked beneath my body, praying to the One who had always carried me through, crying out and seeking refuge. I was down there in the sand for a while, soaked to the bone, waves crashing, creating what would soon be a new coastline. Little did I know the eroding shore would emerge pristine if I just sat still and listened. I released my pain into the universe allowing the tide to carry it out to sea. God is good like that. He moves the earth, excavates, and clears the muddy waters. It doesn't happen overnight. An eroding shoreline takes time to stabilize.

After a good run with my caregiver placement agency, I returned to my roots. Music was where my roots were planted, and I'd always made good money. It was the right time to return to what I knew.

～

BEING in the music industry for over twenty years, "hooking up" with someone in a bar was never my thing. I could tell a million stories from the stage, almost all of which started with a sloppy, drunken, open-mouth kiss from the dance floor to at least a half dozen cars left behind in the parking lot as the band packed up at 3 a.m. The next night the same two people acted as if they didn't even know each other. It never appealed to me.

One night, midweek, I was sitting alone watching TV when a commercial for a dating site announced that they were giving away a "free weekend to find your perfect match." I picked up my laptop and typed the address in the browser. I convinced myself that I would "just look" to see who's out there. No one had to know what I was doing, and I was sure I wouldn't find my "match" on a dating site.

What the hell.

I signed up, set up my profile, picked a decent picture, and looked around. I yawned and clicked from one profile picture to another— one clichéd hook line after another. It bored me to sleep. As the TV blared in the background, I awakened with a slight crick in my neck. It was 3 a.m. I closed the computer and went to bed.

When I woke up to a silent and still house the next morning, I decided to stay in bed for a while. I could work from my laptop from my bed, and no one would be the wiser. It was a light day. Answer a few emails and eventually get some cleaning done around the house and the dreaded grocery shopping. Celia would be home from being at her father's house for a few nights, and I wanted to cook us a nice dinner. I logged on and went straight to my email. The first thing I saw was nothing work-related; however, it was a full page of inquiries from the dating site I signed up with the night before.

Geez, I thought, *there must be some desperate people out there.* Midthought, I paused; *look who's talking, Jill. You signed up for this just like they did.*

As I started to scroll through the fifty-plus emails from different men, there was absolutely no appeal to the process or potential candidates. It was one boring hook line after another: *delete, delete, delete.* I didn't even bother to look at the photo if their introduction was cheesy. *No, thank you,* I thought. I needed to get some work done.

I kept scrolling through the masses of emails from men looking for a date with anyone who would respond when a laid-back subject line caught my attention: "From California to Florida for a Cocktail and Dinner." I stopped and clicked open. I read his bio and checked out the handsome dude in the profile pic. Yes, I needed to get to my work emails, but first, this. I clicked on the message that the handsome guy-in-the-picture sent me. He introduced himself and shared his contact information.

I'm not sure why, but I felt something tug. A butterfly? Maybe. A spark of hope? Eh, hope for what? I wasn't looking for anything. So, what was the feeling? All I could do was allow myself to explore it. First things first: respond.

We sent a few messages back and forth during the workday. His name was Steve. He was fifty-two. He had relocated to the east coast of Florida from California. And we decided to meet in Orlando, which was in the middle for both of us, for a date, on Saturday.

Our meeting spot was set for downtown Orlando; an accessible landmark in the large metro area was the parking garage right off Church Street, a popular downtown area known for its high-end restaurants and bar hopping. The drive east to central Florida was a little over an hour; I was nervous but excited to meet this man I had only texted and emailed with the past few days. I hadn't even spoken to him. My friends thought I was crazy and put a plan in place if I never returned. They would check on me periodically during the evening, and if they didn't hear from me by a specific time, they would alert the authorities. Sure, it was a risk, but I felt very comfortable rolling the dice for some reason.

I'd never been to that area of Orlando before and missed the exit. The traffic through the downtown metro area looked more like a sped-up picture of car lights in an advertisement than the interstate I was driving on—it was dizzying to look at. As dusk fell over the city, the fast-moving cars jutted in and around my small Jeep Liberty. I didn't have a GPS at the time, and the directions I'd printed out were useless as I couldn't take my eyes off the road. I had no choice but to call Steve. I pulled onto the shoulder and clicked on his number.

"Hello?" The voice on the other end was smiling; I could see it through the phone. His voice moved me. Like a warm blanket, it felt like home.

"Hi...Steve?" I smiled back. "It's Jill."

I nervously laughed as I admitted I was lost.

"Hey there. No problem, I'll guide you." He sounded like safety. It was a feeling I'd never felt before. My anxiety and embarrassment began to wane. His directions were seamless. He guided me straight to him.

I pulled into the parking garage, there he stood. Tall and handsome, dirty blond hair with some gray mixed in. He wore wire-rimmed glasses like Kevin Costner in JFK. However, he looked like a younger Eric Clapton. My heart was pounding. I couldn't park fast enough. Steve waited for me at the entrance of the four-story parking garage. I looked in the rearview mirror, checked my hair, smacked my lips together, and never looked back. Our date lasted eight hours; eight hours turned into a lifetime.

CHAPTER 10

Love is love is love.
~Lin Manuel Miranda

~

*W*e both swore we would never do it again. But there we were on the beach at sunset in one of the most beautiful places on earth, Key West, Florida, vowing to love each other for the rest of our lives. Steve asked me to marry him exactly one year to the day of our first date: February 4, 2013. It was magical and romantic. After three failed marriages and barely memorable proposals, Steve made up for it. His proposal was the only one that counted. He had it all planned and arranged ahead of time. I would find out after the engagement that Steve bought the ring a few months earlier and waited for our first anniversary to roll around. From dinner reservations to the perfect wine/food pairing and the proposal. It was the fairy tale I'd waited forty-three years for. He planned and executed the moment well.

Over our year-long courtship, we built a healthy relationship on friendship, love, and trust. It was what we considered to be a long-distance relationship. We lived on opposite sides of Florida, about a hundred miles one way. We saw each other every weekend and once during the week if our schedules allowed. It worked, and I learned what unconditional love looked like. Our relationship was mutual and grounded in respect for each other. I'd never experienced anything like that before.

As we discussed our impending nuptials, since we both had been married more than once, we decided to elope and wanted to do it sooner than later.

"I didn't ask you to marry me to wait, Jill. I want you to be my wife," he said.

No one had ever said that to me before. Out of the three men I'd married, not one of them ever looked at me and stated so emphatically they wanted me to be their wife. I would have a husband, a family, and unconditional love. Something I'd longed for my entire life. We set the date a little over a month from his proposal.

IT WAS UNSEASONABLY cold in Key West when we arrived a few days before our wedding. The typically warm, spring winds felt more like an arctic chill for being less than two thousand miles north of the equator. The wind ripped through the tiny island, and we did not come prepared with the right wardrobe. Instead of bikinis, tank tops, and shorts, we needed long sleeves, jackets, and scarves. Off to Ross we went and purchased an entire winter wardrobe (Florida style) for the duration of the trip. We also started to worry about our upcoming beach ceremony. We'd hired a local husband-and-wife team to perform the ceremony and take the wedding photos at sunset standing on the shore where the Gulf of Mexico meets the Atlantic Ocean. We would have to wait and see what the next few days would bring.

The days preceding the wedding were cold and rainy. The weather report didn't show much change the entire week we were there, including the day of the ceremony. We didn't care; we could get married anywhere, our hotel room if needed.

Much to our surprise, the morning of our wedding, we awoke to cloudless blue skies and mild temperatures in the mid-70s after days of low 50s. Fingers crossed, the weather would continue to cooperate through sunset. And it did.

March 8, 2013. The day was flawless. There's no doubt that God crafted this day with the two of us in mind. As we waited in the hotel lobby for our ride to the ceremony, I looked at the man standing in front of me, the man who would soon be my husband, dressed in crisp, ironed, khaki linen pants and a white linen shirt, gazing at me with his piercing blue eyes, I thought to myself: *What did I do to deserve his love? I must have done something good.*

It wasn't long before I was humming remnants of Julie Andrews and Christopher Plummer's famous duet from my favorite childhood movie, *The Sound of Music*: "Something Good."

Eloping was the way to go—Just the two of us, no stress, no money spent on everyone else's desires, no distractions, no drama. The ceremony was perfect, and so was my new husband. He was (and still is) the most handsome man I've ever laid eyes on. He's also the kindest. The space of chaos where I once lived, I'd outgrown, moved on. For the year we dated, Steve showed me what calm looked like. Steve is my Grand Canyon, the beautiful place I never thought I'd witness. He is home: a cozy space—my chicken soup—I like to call him.

∾

I was no longer Jill Wilson, yet I identified with her more than ever. I realize that my entire life was spent running away from her. Throughout my life and many marriages, I thought changing my name would change my past and the shame it was tethered to. I had always hoped a new husband would equal a new life and somehow erase the pain of my past and the grounding trauma. I was wrong. I had to love myself first.

Over the years, my last name changed more than some people changed their driver's license address. I lived most of my adult life ashamed of the multiple marriages, name changes, and fucked-up choices that felt like one big backfire after another.

Marrying Steve didn't scare me, and I was proud to take his name. Along with a new last name came my knowing. Knowing I was where I was supposed to be. It had been a lifetime of not knowing, and, finally, the knowing grounded me at my core. I allowed healing to take place. The newness felt like what I imagine a newborn feels after the first breath of life. Without being aware of their surroundings, the inherent sense of knowing it's safe to breathe, and the freedom from a confined space. I could move and stretch in my new environment.

It took me forty-three years to learn how to breathe and to feel the sense of calm that washed over me every time I exhaled. I was Jill Carlyle: new, improved, whole, knowing for the first time in my life that I belonged. There was something about the name change that was a rebirth. Or maybe it was that I had just never been able to take a breath until then.

Unfortunately, the one person I had hoped would be happy for me was unsure of my choice to marry Steve. It wasn't Steve's undoing of trust or a case of dislike; I had to own her issue. My past preceded my future, and although my daughter tried to be happy for me, my past decisions ruined her faith in me and my ability to make good choices when it came to men and especially marriages. Our already strained relationship was stretched thinner each day. Celia congratulated us on our engagement, even helped me choose my wedding dress, but her true feelings would reveal themselves right after she graduated from high school in June 2013.

Everything I did (or didn't do) made her angry. A mirror image of the feelings I had for my own mother. The ice was paper-thin; no matter how lightly I would tread, there was always a piece that would crack, and I'd fall feet first into the icy cold river of Celia.

I don't blame her for doubting my decision to marry Steve. I don't even blame her for her anger and resentment. Looking back, I feel my relationship with men was a trigger for her PTSD, a slap in the face and blatant reminder of the many times I put a man before her. In her mind, I was repeating the behaviors of her childhood. She didn't trust me. I understood that. I just hoped she would allow me to show her that this time, this man, this love was different. But I tried too hard. I didn't allow Celia to take things at her own pace. I shoved the marriage and my expectations of her behavior and what I thought her emotional response should be down her throat, and she rejected all my efforts.

That part of my life, the lost relationship with my daughter, was emotionally disruptive. It was a pain that bordered (borders) on unbearable. But for the first time in my life, for the first time I remember, I could call myself happy. Without Celia in my life, I wasn't whole, but I was happy from my center. My twenty-year-old son and I were on good terms, and my marriage was something I had only dreamed about. Within weeks of Celia graduating, I moved from my rented two-bedroom townhouse in a lovely area of east Hillsborough County (Tampa Bay) called Fishhawk Ranch, where both of my children graduated from high school. I permanently relocated to the central-eastern coast of Florida with my new husband. After living in the Tampa Bay area for thirty-plus years, the move was a welcome change. It was time to start fresh.

～

IN THE EARLY months of our marriage, all we could afford was a small two-bedroom apartment in a lovely part of town. I didn't care where we lived as long as we were together.

Steve was in the same boat; he was starting over as well. That's why our relationship worked. We were both in a place of resetting and committed to doing it as a team. He worked long hours for a local general contracting company as their chief estimator. Although he'd been in the construction business for over thirty years, he was rebuilding his career from the ground up after relocating from California (where he closed his own contracting company).

"Give it time and patience. I promise you it won't be like this forever," Steve would tell me from time to time when I questioned him about the hours he was putting in versus the lack of compensation he was earning for his effort. I didn't care where we lived or how much was in the bank; I just hated seeing him so tired and frustrated at times.

So we made a plan. Steve would dive into his career as the chief estimator for a hugely successful contractor. I would go to college and supplement my income by continuing to "gig" as a solo artist at various venues in Central Florida. It was a great job, quick money, and work hours were in the evenings and on weekends. Perfect for the student life, even if I was considered the "non-traditional student." I learned to bypass that title and make the most out of the opportunities I created for myself. It had been a journey to get to that point. I was ready to put everything in place.

CHAPTER 11

Don't spend all of your time trying to find yourself. Spend your time creating yourself into a person that you'll be proud of.
~Sonja Parker

I'd never experienced freedom *from myself* before. I finally had choices. I didn't have to lie on applications anymore, and I could finally plan the educational journey I'd dreamed of for years.

Two months after Steve and I married, with my GED in hand, I proudly registered at the local campus of Eastern Florida State College. Within a month of registering, I found myself sitting in my first college class. I felt a sense of pride that I had never felt before.

Yet I continued to struggle with the distant fact that I was a high school dropout. My learned behavior was that the reputation associated with high school dropouts is that of "loser." That was engraved in my brain. *I am a loser*. Not to mention, I was still living a lie. I still hadn't told my husband that I was a high school dropout.

The idea that I had not been forthcoming with Steve about a part of my life shook me. We had built a relationship built on honesty and trust. Our past relationships had been grounded in dysfunction, leaving us both numb to the idea of ever marrying again. But our relationship turned out to be something we'd never experienced before. Although we had plenty of marriages under our belt, ours was like getting a do-over, erasing the past, and starting back at square one. Yet the inherent fear of telling him the truth stirred up the words my mother had said to me over and over as a teenager, young adult, and young wife, "Don't ever tell anyone, especially a man, that you quit school, had an abortion, or that you were married at sixteen. No one will ever want to be with you. No one wants to be with a quitter, and no man wants a wife who's made as many mistakes as you have. A woman with baggage will always be left on the side of the road."

I heard rejection. I couldn't handle any more rejection. I was finally married to an amazing man; I couldn't risk losing him. But I couldn't take the dishonesty I'd brought into our marriage any longer. I had to tell him. Although I still felt like an imposter at times, I completed my freshman year of college at almost forty-four years old with straight As. I was getting stronger, and my past was moving farther away from my future. I knew that I needed to own it to heal from my past. My husband needed to know. Maybe the confessional and my recent accomplishments would be enough for him to overlook the information I chose to withhold. It felt like a game of Russian Roulette.

It took me a few tries to find the courage to reveal the secret I'd been keeping. Not only because I had lied to him by making him believe that I was a high school graduate but also because I'd never spoken that truth out loud. I had never said the words "I never graduated from high school" to anyone for fear of rejection, name-calling, disappointment, judgment. The centerpiece of my childhood. That was the culture I was born into: judge, laugh, taunt, reject, hate, abandon.

One night when we were out to dinner, I finally disclosed my shameful secret to my new husband. Trying to get the words out was nearly impossible. The despair on Steve's face was evident as I tried to deliver what I considered damning information.

"What, Jill?" He said breathlessly with the concern of someone bracing themselves for devastating news, "Just tell me, what are you trying to say? Whatever it is, I can handle it."

I paused; tears were streaming down my face, "Steve, I never graduated from high school." I was filled with such shame; I couldn't even look at him.

We were sitting at a high-top table at one of our favorite waterfront restaurants. My hands were folded over the bread plate catching the crumbs of my past. I cowered like a scolded puppy and twirled my thumbs. Before I could look up, my husband's hands covered mine.

I'm safe, I thought to myself. I slowly lifted my heavy head to meet his eyes.

"That's what you were afraid to tell me? That you didn't graduate from high school?" He asked.

"Yes, I didn't graduate from high school. And I'm sorry I lied to you. I love you, and I don't want to lose you, and I'm sorry I lied. I'm ashamed, Steve. I'm ashamed of my past. Not graduating from high school is one of my biggest regrets." I was still feeling extremely insecure, not sure what he was feeling.

"Baby, this is what you couldn't tell me? Why?" He asked.

I felt like a child. Not because he was making me feel like one, but I transported back to my troubled teenage years and the many conversations that centered around the embarrassment and shame I brought to my family—the belittling of my spirit, the sinking quicksand that sucked the identity from my person. I listened to those that were supposed to love me unconditionally, tell me time and time again that I was a disappointment, and demanded I believe that living in my shame was my eternal punishment. Disappointing others meant abandonment, and abandonment ended in solitude. The trauma-induced triggers of my past were clear.

My husband held my hands inside of his for a moment without saying a word. The silence spoke volumes. As I brought myself back to the present, I began to understand the weight of the inherent shame I felt as I replayed our conversation in my mind. For the first time, perhaps, ever, I began to separate myself from my trauma. I was abused by the one person who should have been protecting me: my mother. Posthumously, her words still tormented my conscience.

Disclosing the truth to Steve set me free. It was a step closer to my healing journey. Over the next four years, I soared to new personal and academic heights: I earned my AA in education and graduated with honors. I was accepted into the University of Central Florida, where I finished my bachelor's degree in English literature with a concentration in pedagogical writing and rhetoric, graduating magna cum laude.

At the beginning of my educational journey, I never expected to go any farther than my insecurities and self-doubts would take me. Once I was nearing the end of my undergraduate program, I started thinking about pursuing a master's degree. The summer before my senior year in the English and Writing program at UCF, I applied to work as a peer tutor in the writing center on campus. I opted to take online classes for the better part of my time at UCF, but I yearned for the college campus experience. I didn't care if I was forty-six years old, I wanted to be a part of something larger, those with the same mindset, so I registered for on-campus classes in the fall of my senior year and went through the rigorous application process to be accepted as a writing specialist on campus in the writing center.

There were so many moments I questioned myself. Wasn't it

enough that I was in college? How ridiculous was I to be inserting myself into a world with the younger generation? Really? What the fuck was I doing? Was I having a midlife crisis? Trying to live vicariously through these young people? How would I relate to them? With them? What would they think of me? Most of them were younger than my grown children.

I allowed courage to lead. I deleted society's rules and constructs surrounding the mindset of the aging woman, quelled my insecurities, stopped asking unhelpful questions of myself, and did the thing. To work in the writing center, candidates had to have two letters of recommendation from a former professor or administrator, produce a writing sample, a letter of intent, and an in-person interview with the center's director. Once accepted, candidates were required to take a graduate-level writing course and work at least fifteen hours a week tutoring students across all disciplines and levels from undergrad to doctoral. These requirements were above and beyond the students' regular schedules. I could handle it. At my age, I knew this would be my only opportunity to fulfill my desire for the college experience that I'd longed for my entire life and gain experience at the same time.

I was accepted into the program and prepared myself for a challenging semester. I was a forty-six-year-old college senior with two semesters left. I had a lot to make up for in a short period.

The day I walked into the Writing Center for the mandatory orientation, I was greeted and treated as an equal. I made friends being a part of the Writing Center team and in other face-to-face classes that I attended. I forged lifelong friends that, to this day, I stay in contact with.

Those amazing young people are a big part of why I considered graduate school in the final year of my undergraduate program. Most of my colleagues from the Writing Center were either master's students or doctoral candidates. We spent a lot of time together between our shifts at the center and our evening class that met for three hours twice a week. We laughed together, cheered each other on, were horrified, and cried when Donald Trump was elected president and protested in solidarity over issues that we advocated for and against. They were all intelligent and driven, and their drive inspired me to keep going.

My heart was set on applying to one school: the University of Miami. This was my family's alma mater: my uncle and oldest brother played football for the U, and my nephew attended his undergraduate program there. Back in the 70s, my father was a general contractor and built many of the buildings on campus. The ties ran deep, and the family bled orange and green (even if you didn't want to). There hadn't been a woman in our family who had attended the U, and I wanted to be the first.

Although I loved the school, more so, I loved the idea of being accepted into the same school that the successful and well-respected members of my family attended. I thought if they discovered that I, too, was good enough to be accepted into and graduate from the University of Miami, they would finally accept me. That school was a "status" symbol in my family, and those that had attended the school were highly esteemed and respected in the Wilson lineage. Maybe I would belong in the family for the first time in my existence. Perhaps I would even deserve the namesake, the one I'd been running from my entire life (or was it the one I'd been running to?) I went through the rigorous application process. I wrote my personal statement, retrieved glowing recommendations from former professors punctuated by my undergraduate academic standing of 3.97. I looked good on paper.

I waited patiently once all the required components were submitted to the acceptance board. The feeling of anticipation was familiar: accomplishment, making others proud, and longing for accolades from my family, who ignored my existence for most of my adult life. I was constantly digging up hope that my family would one day accept me. When was I going to yearn for self-acceptance? Perhaps the real issue here isn't the validity of the people who had shunned me but my own validation.

About a week later, I received the call, and an official letter of acceptance from the University of Miami: *Dear Jill, You have been accepted into the Master of Communication Science program at the University of Miami...*

I couldn't believe my eyes. I reached another milestone, one I had earned with hard work, patience, and perseverance. Indeed, now, I would be accepted into the family. But they would never know. I wanted so badly to tell my sister. *This would undoubtedly connect us,* I thought. Maybe even reunite us. A fantasy that played out in my mind with the fairytale ending wouldn't happen. At least not right then. My husband and I celebrated my accomplishment, and I finished up the two months remaining of my undergrad at UCF. We planned a nice graduation celebration despite the absence of my family.

The graduation announcements had been sent out, the venue secured, cake ordered, the last thing left to do was pick up my cap and gown. Outside of the commencement, the day I picked up my regalia was one of the most emotional days of my life. It was like seeing my newborn baby for the first time after a four-year pregnancy and challenging delivery. Crazy visual, but that's what it felt like. I could barely choke back the tears.

"Name, please?" the student volunteer asked.

"Jill Suzanne Carlyle." My voice was shaky, and I kept my dark sunglasses on to hide the waterfall of tears I was desperately trying to hold back.

She handed me the plastic bag with all the necessary items for graduation day and return instructions. The cap and tassel were for me to keep, but the gown was to be returned after the ceremony.

"Wait." The young girl motioned me back to her table. "You're magna cum laude. See that line over there?" She pointed toward the other side of the room, where the lines were much shorter than the one I had been waiting in.

I nodded yes.

"That is where you pick up your honors cords and instructions on where you will be seated during the commencement ceremony." She smiled and helped the next graduate.

I took a deep breath. I floated toward the line. A part of me felt foolish, out of time, a little too late for all this hoopla. I was forty-seven years old.

This is for the young kids, I thought.

No. This was for anyone, at any age that earned it. And I earned it.

THE HARD CEMENT floor was crowded with soon-to-be graduates cloaked in heavy black robes tapered in gold—our school's colors. From where I was standing, all I could see were the backs of artistically crafted caps with all kinds of crazy (and creative) little sayings like "She Believed She Could So She Did" and "Finally!" and "I'm Poor!" Most of these pending graduates were the age of my children—but that didn't stop me. Nothing did. It was finally time, the day I had waited for my entire life but never thought I would see: the day that I, a high school dropout, would be graduating magna cum laude from a major university.

The powerful "Pomp and Circumstance" filled the large, airy arena; I couldn't believe that I was there. The music reached the very core of my being, rebounding off the roots of the dysfunction I thought I would never escape. I kept waiting to awaken from the most empowering dream I'd ever had. This moment wasn't a dream; it was reality. As the tears welled in the corners of my eyes, I tried like hell to brush it off: wiggled my nose, cleared my throat, looked down, then up, trying to turn the water off. Lightheaded, I nearly collapsed.

Hold it together, Jill. This is your moment—all yours. You earned every piece and part of right now.

The line of graduates was dense. We proceeded, and even though my feet were starting to throb from the six-inch stilettos, I couldn't feel anything but pride. As we made our way from the crowded corridor into the arena, a cold gush of air hit me as I walked over the threshold—a force of wind so strong it filled my lungs with their presence: they were there, my mom and dad— not in the flesh but the spirit—whispering, that they were proud of me.

For the first time, I allowed myself to believe them.

I looked up, and to the left into the crowd of cheering families, I spotted my husband, a big smile reaching wide across his face, beaming with pride. Standing alongside him, my in-laws, who'd only known me for a few years, waved with the love of parents who had birthed me. On the left side of Steve stood my lifelong best friend, Danielle. The only part of my past that showed up in the flesh. Those people. Their presence. They are home.

As I followed the young man in front of me, my entire life played out in slow motion like the reel of an old-time movie. I looked down at the dark, slick floor. I felt the cold hardness against the sole of my shoes, reminding me of the words I'd heard spoken over and over behind my back and to my face—words I grew up believing—words that were a packed vehicle of shame and fear that drove my life for many years.

"Jill, she'll never amount to anything."

"She's so pretty; it's too bad she's so screwed-up."

The years of being the laughingstock of the Wilson family, the taunting, the exclusion from family functions, the gossip, the social media blocking, the insults spewed from the mouth of my adult niece as she gave my mother's eulogy at her funeral, passive-aggressively attacking me for the way I "daughtered" took their toll. These people with whom I shared the same DNA controlled my thoughts for most of my life. I believed them when they showed me I was unimportant, didn't belong, wasn't good enough to represent the Wilson name, and wasn't part of the lineage I was born into. These thoughts swirled round and round in my head as I walked toward my seat.

My seat where the other honor graduates are sitting, those that earned the title of summa cum laude and magna cum laude.

My alma mater, the family of which I was now a part of—a family lineage not born of blood but hard work, dedication, passion, and persistence. I finally had a seat at the table. So, this is what it feels like. This is what belonging feels like.

There were moments I still doubted my worth, but I wasn't going to allow the haunting of my own blood to suck any more of my thoughts. They didn't deserve another minute of me. I pushed the insignificant thoughts and people out of the way; I arrived at my seat, took a deep breath, praised God for His grace, and looked up at the stage. The University of Central Florida. There in black and gold, the colossal UCF Pegasus emblem hung from the rafters. At forty-seven years old, I did it. I was graduating from college.

As I began the short, but very long journey, from my seat to the stage where the president of my soon-to-be alma mater would award me the highest distinction I'd ever earned, my heart raced as my mind replayed the events that got me there: patience —the mindset never to give up. I recalled the sneers from family members at the very sight of me; I remembered the gossip and whispers behind my back that went on for years (and continue by many to this day). My heart began to sink as I allowed these thoughts to fill the cracks and crevices of my heart. But as I walked up the side stairs that hoisted me onto the stage of mentors who helped me achieve my goals, I held my head high, the toxic noise of my flesh and blood began to dissipate. I began to hum along to the music; I breathed in every moment, allowing pride to fill every square inch of my inner being—my lifeline—I was alive and proud. The roots of shame were excavating.

CHAPTER 12

She is clothed in strength and dignity, and she laughs without fear of the future.
~Proverbs 31:25

I wouldn't be here today if my faith in Christ were nonexistent. Through some of my darkest days, marriages, divorces, death, and loss, had my faith wavered, I would not have survived. My God gave (and still does) me hope and promise. In one of my favorite books, *Jesus Feminist*, author Sara Bessey prefaces chapter 1 with the following excerpt by Oxford scholar Dorothy Sayers from the essay "Are Women Human?"

> Perhaps it is no wonder that the women were first at the Cradle and last at the Cross. They had never known a man like this Man —there never has been another. A prophet and teacher who never nagged at them, never flattered or coaxed or patronized; who never made arch jokes about them, never treated them as

"The Women; God help us!" or "The ladies, God Bless them!";
who rebuked without querulousness and praised without conde-
scension; who took their questions and arguments seriously; who
never mapped out their sphere for them, never urged them to be
feminine or jeered at them for being female; who had no ax to
grind and no uneasy male dignity to defend; who took them as he
found them and was completely unselfconscious. There is no act,
no sermon, no parable in the whole Gospel that borrows its
pungency from female perversity; nobody could guess from the
words and deeds of Jesus that there was anything "funny"
about woman's nature.

There isn't a more accurate passage written about the man
Jesus was. And whoever Jesus is to you, Savior, prophet, histor-
ical figure, he was not any of the things that fall under patriarchy's umbrella: misogynistic, sexist, a socially constructed ego,
condescending, controlling, unforgiving, demeaning, insulting,
and demoralizing. And he wasn't white. As a young girl growing
up in the 70s and 80s, the dome of patriarchy housed the culture
in which I was raised. I thought it was normal to live under the
rules and regulations of a man intersecting with the ideology of
religion. "Man of the house" was a term loosely thrown around
my childhood; gender lines were drawn. That was *my* normal.

I was raised in the quintessential culture of the ultimate privileged white Christian male world in a household where women
were secondary. Males in our family took precedence over
females. Men were revered and celebrated; women were judged
and objectified. While the boys were raised and prepped for
athletics, higher education, and the military, the girls were
groomed for marriage and babies.

Being raised in a religious home is a far cry from being raised
in a spiritual one. Looking back, the behaviors they referred to as
Christian and philanthropic were, to me, the veil hiding their
true identity. They could not forgive, understand, and empathize

with those that were different and carried differing opinions and behaviors that revealed the ugly core of my bloodline.

I couldn't see through the blindfold that was tightly secured over my eyes from my very first breath. The irony was that subconsciously, as a child, none of it felt right, yet I didn't know how to put my finger on the pulse of what was skewed. I reacted instead of acted. I rebelled. Not only in my childhood but also in my relationships with partners, friends, family, especially my kids.

Growing up I was never given the tools to cope with people who had differing opinions and belief systems because I didn't have an identity of my own. While my family was trying to construct who they thought I should be, I was doing my damnedest to figure out who the fuck I was and where I might find her. All the while still trying to bond with people that would never accept me, regardless of what my future would hold. They became jealous and hateful when they couldn't create a "Jill" that fit their ideas and justify their pathetic behavior.

I do not speak to anyone in my family. Yes, it makes me sad sometimes, but it also set me free. I don't have to accept their idea of "me" just because we share the same DNA.

MY PARENTS DID ALL THE "THINGS" the societal Christian was supposed to do. I was a victim, and ultimately a survivor, of religious tradition. Although I never conformed to what those around me claimed was acceptable, it taught me that God's love is always present, even though my family, and the world surrounding me, were cold and cruel. God spoke to me at a very young age without uttering a word and planted hope at my center.

Every Sunday, we went to church and were taught to fear the Lord because he was a man, and men wielded power. The word "fear" was connoted in every conversation, confrontation and rooted so deeply inside of me that it became inherent. Women were subservient, and I was taught to obey and fear the authority of a man. Especially my father.

"Your father will be home from work any minute, Jill. When he gets home, you will tell him what you did. He will deal with you," my mother would threaten when I was in trouble on her watch. And I always knew I would get the belt. My mother rarely did the dirty work. She awarded that to my father. The vicious cycle would start: fear-driven anxiety, flight mode activated, more anxiety, more fear.

The perpetual question: *How can I get out of this? How can I make this not as bad as my mother is making it out to be?* I would ask myself. I learned to live in fear, especially of a man's reaction, to devise and deliver stories to get out of whatever predicament I'd gotten myself into, so I was deemed good enough to be loved. Lying was habitual because I couldn't be myself or tell the truth without the fear of being emotionally abolished for just being me. I learned to become someone I wasn't and became someone I didn't know in the process.

I never agreed with my parents' opinions, but I was born imbued within a racist culture. That was my exposure, and it took me years of educating myself to unpack the truth. Recently, a family member shared a disturbing story about a few of my brother's black University of Miami teammates who came to the house one day for a cookout and swim in the family pool. After they left, my father (at my mother's request) wanted the pool drained. This was the disgust of the culture I was born into.

That was my normal for years, yet I knew something was wrong with that mindset. I was never introduced to humanity; that word was never used in our household. The only living beings that were deemed "humans" were white people. Growing up, culture meant "white culture," the only culture that counted in my father's world.

I WAS THRUST into adulthood wearing dark sunglasses and blinders to shield the extra light that tried to peek through. I thought it was customary to rely on a man for my happiness. As a young adult, I believed that being married, having children, cooking, cleaning, and making myself beautiful for my husband constituted my life's purpose. Conversely, those ideals never fit the identity that was clawing its way out in my first three marriages. I was only told a single story of life.

I knew nothing of feminism until my sophomore year of college at the ripe age of forty-four. Everything that I had been exposed to my entire life began to unravel like the plot of a good mystery; I started uncovering opinions of my own. Opinions that had been suffocated by oppression the first forty-three years of my life. Not only did I have my own thoughts, but I knew why I had the views I did.

My identity was no longer grounded in shame, and I realized God still loved me. Today, my faith is stronger than it's ever been. I don't play into religion's rules. And I no longer question God's love for me. I am a Christian, yet I don't subscribe to society's construct of Christianity. I am deeply spiritual, but I am not religious. I love God on the terms we set—not on a church's expectations.

I GREW UP A SINGLE STORY, only seeing one dimension of everything, including myself. I had no idea what a three-dimensional life looked like until I reached my mid-forties. I missed so much of life because I was trying to survive (and figure out) "my self." I was told the single-story over and over; here's the laundry list:

- Look pretty
- "Always make sure you are 'done-up' when your husband gets home from work," my mother would say
- Keep your opinions to yourself
- Agree with your husband (especially if he's paying all the bills)
- Do what you're told
- Dreams are not reality
- Your value and worth are based on the man you marry (and the success of the marriage).
- Don't stand out
- Lie. Keep secrets, so people don't judge you
- Hide your mistakes (the words "transparency" wasn't in my vocabulary)
- Know how to change a tire (this is the only decent piece of advice in this entire list)

Had I known I was more than a single story, I wouldn't have fought against myself and everyone else for so many years.

All that changed when I realized there was a bigger, more diverse world and that diversity and culture were (is) the center-piece of humanity. Once I started college, everything shifted, especially my mindset. As an English major, I had access to a wide range of courses and took as many as possible. I wanted a taste of it all. I took classes on everything from England's Restoration-era to Black Literary Studies, to a Survey of Jane Austen and American Literature, dating as far back as the seventeenth century. But there was one particular genre that tugged at my soul: Women's Literature. My memoir wouldn't be complete without acknowledging how profoundly studying women's words throughout history changed my life. I credit two classes that impacted everything about my past and present and set the trajectory of my future self.

I'd completed three semesters at the University of Central

Florida but still had three to go. My advisor suggested I take two condensed literature classes during the summer so I could graduate the following spring. She highly recommended the names of two tenured professors that taught courses within the discipline of women and gender studies as they intersected with literature.

"I know you have a strong interest in women's studies, Jill." My advisor said as we discussed my schedule for the summer term.

"I do."

"I'm going to register you for Women Writers with Dr. Lisa Logan and Women Writers of Color with Farrah Cato. Both are fully online, six-week summer terms. They are condensed, and fast-paced, but you will love them. I have no doubt you will thrive. These professors are two of the college's best."

"Sign me up!"

Over the next twelve weeks, I was awakened. I started seeing the world through the lens of an independent woman—a woman holding the rights to her own identity. I eased into feminist ideology the same way I eased into my oldest and most comfortable pair of jeans. The kind of jeans that just fit no matter how long you've owned, washed, or worn them.

I remember the first time I heard the term "female agency." It was my second semester at UCF, and I was taking Restoration Literature. RL is a literary response to the social and political upheavals of the English Civil War, the regicide of King Charles I, and the restraints endured during the eleven years of Puritan rule under the Commonwealth (and Protectorate) governance. Women of that era were discouraged (and even forbidden) to use their voices or pen their stories. To make a living as a writer, a woman often used a pen name to cloak her identity as a female. More male writers were studied than females, but what I loved about this course were the solid female writers of the time. My professor, Dr. Kate Oliver, grounded our studies of this male-centric era in the female agency, illuminating powerful women through the work of Aphra Behn, the first professional woman writer in England. "Agency" is what Behn championed in her work: "the intellectual capacity of women to make intelligent, purposive decisions, under standard constraints that face most decision-makers."

Whoa. I was in search of my agency, and I was damn well going to find it. Since discovering her, I haven't stopped talking about the seventeenth-century poet, playwright, and fiction writer. Her legacy propels my work forward and reminds me of the fierceness that is the female voice.

The summer courses following my Restoration Lit class solidified everything for me. I no longer had to attach myself to the ideals, favorites, and opinions of the family that had detached themselves from me thirty years prior. I soaked up everything, every word of every woman's story that I read, researched, and wrote about. These women became my SHEros, my mentors, and my cheerleaders, and yet they'd never even met me. Their work gave me hope, taught me lessons, and empowered me to use my voice to help empower other women. I realized that women had wasted centuries fighting against each other instead of leaning in and lifting each other up, and we are all a part of a sisterhood, and glass ceilings are meant to be broken.

Throughout my studies, these women taught me things about myself I wouldn't have discovered on my own: Audre Lorde taught me that my silence won't protect me; Dr. Brene Brown told me to brave the wilderness; Alice Walker encouraged me to not give up my power by thinking I didn't have any; Sandra Cisneros made me see that I'm too powerful, too beautiful, too sure of who I am to deserve anything less; Oprah Winfrey challenged me to root for my own rise, and Glennon Doyle showed me that I am a "goddamn cheetah."

CHAPTER 13

You own everything that happened to you. Tell your stories. If people wanted you to write warmly about them, they should have behaved better.
~Anne Lamott

Two months after completing my bachelor's degree from the University of Central Florida, I began online classes within the Communication Sciences program at the University of Miami. Although my writing background came in handy, and I was attending what I thought was the school of my dreams, my heart wasn't fulfilled. I missed analyzing literature and writing stories. I missed the craft of writing.

I was intent on earning my master's degree from the University of Miami. After all, this was the school I'd pined over my entire life. The school that my family hailed as the pinnacle of educational achievement and that only the family's finest "men" had ever attended. "It's all about the U" was ingrained and replayed in my head my entire life. I convinced myself that I would be revered and accepted as a "Wilson" if I could get at least one of my degrees from that particular college, even though the degree program had nothing to do with my original career choice. I wanted to write books, empower women, and eventually become a professor and teach writing on the college level.

Because of my nagging childhood dream to graduate from UM, I struggled with the decision to leave the program, but more so the school. I thought and rethought things, analyzed every situation, and concluded this wasn't an academic issue. It was grounded in shame; once again, I was trying to do something to make my family proud. I thought there was more "fixing of shame" to be done. But then I realized they wouldn't care anyway. I needed to make my decisions for me, not for the people I was only connected to by blood. Because in this case, blood was not thicker than water. I needed to fix my shame for me and learn to love and accept the woman God always intended me to be.

After the first semester, I withdrew from the University of Miami and began looking for a graduate English and/or creative writing program. I took my time, did my research, stayed in academia, and enrolled in the Women and Gender Studies master's certificate program at my alma mater, the University of Central Florida. During that time, I eventually earned additional graduate-level credits that I planned on applying toward a Ph.D. I applied to Southern New Hampshire University and pursued a double master's degree in English and Creative Nonfiction. That was one of the best academic decisions I ever made. I was finally building my identity and peeling back the layers, reintroducing me to myself, and learning how to write my story.

∾

THE NONFICTION CREATIVE Writing curriculum at SNHU centered around a work-in-progress manuscript culminating (over two years) in a master's thesis, which I defended as my final degree requirement. That is to say, the nonfiction creative writing courses I took alongside the literary courses, assisted in scaffolding my project from beginning to nearly the end of my manuscript.

I'd been wrestling with the idea of writing my story for a few years. But the idea started to take shape as I began the journey into midlife. I was forty-seven years old, and in four years, I'd earned my high school diploma, associate's degree, and bachelor's degree and had been accepted into two graduate programs at highly respected schools. I was coming into myself, resetting, and able to reflect on my past and sort through the pain. Writing about it helped me do that—writing my story as I progressed through graduate school felt right. I'd spent four and a half years in college and was conditioned to writing academic essays, so the creative guidance I gained helped me craft my story ideas and shape my writing voice. I brought my threadbare manuscript into the program, and from there, I began the long journey into *Finding Fifty*.

MY MEMOIR IS SO MUCH MORE than a simple recount of my traumatic childhood and poor choices as an adult. It served as a personal excavation tool. I had no idea how writing about the things so deeply rooted in shame would help me find the identity I'd been void of my entire life. The many rewrite, revisions, and drafts this manuscript has gone through symbolize how far I've come and the work that I was sometimes blind to. It also tells me I will always be a work in progress.

When I finally reached the last semester of my master's program, I was fifteen thousand words shy of the thirty-thousand-word thesis requirement. I had more to write; I just didn't realize I had it in me. After six years of school, I was exhausted, but I kept going. I muddled my way through, received decent feedback, made a near-perfect score, and defended it. But there was still so much more work to be done. The shell was there, but it was time for the inside work. I knew once I could write from the inside out instead of the other way around, not only would my story resonate with others, but it would resonate with me.

IN THE SUMMER OF 2020, during some of the darkest times of the COVID-19 pandemic, I completed a double master's degree in English and Nonfiction Creative Writing with a 3.99 GPA. Since earning my undergraduate degree and throughout my masters, I'd taught middle school English and academic and creative writing to international middle and high school students. Life was busier than ever, and I continued to work on my manuscript. However, the deeper I'd dig, the farther away from finishing I found myself. I was questioning every word I put on the page. I questioned my writing, my stories, my truth. Every time I sat down to write, I ran headfirst into the side of a mountain. I felt like I didn't deserve to tell my story. Imposter syndrome took over and I was stuck. I still had more "stuff" to tread through.

AS THE PANDEMIC globally ravaged humanity, I reconciled with my sister after not speaking with her for over a decade (and barely speaking to her for years prior). I thought our newfound relationship as adults would be healing. On the contrary, although I didn't realize it at the time, the reconciliation and spending time with her subconsciously brought back the toxicity I'd worked for years to purge.

She reached out first. In the early months of the pandemic, the lockdown allowed only a daily trip to the end of the driveway to the mailbox. It felt like Groundhog Day. Same driveway, different day, same bills, different week. Although my aunt clued me in a few days before my sister had written to me, an electric shock ran through my body when I saw her name on the return address.

The letter was heavier than a standard letter, with a few extra stamps stuck in the upper right-hand corner of the envelope. I needed to sit in my own space and read the words she'd written to me. I was in a neutral, almost numb, frame of mind as I ripped open the flap secured with extra tape. The letter was cordial. The tone, taciturn—exactly how I remember my sister. But she reached out to me after years of keeping every bit of distance she could. Even though I was unsure of her reasoning, I felt a sense of belonging. I'd longed to have a relationship with my sister. For years, I dreamed of saying, "my sister and me..." and building memories we'd never had the chance to make. But this was just a letter. I tried not to get my hopes up, and I was still sitting in the liminal space between feeling and numb.

I didn't have much of an internal response. I read the letter to my husband.

"Are you going to write her back?" He asked.

"At some point," I said.

I didn't know what to say because I didn't know how to feel.

I finally found the words to say to her. A few days later, I replied to her letter reintroducing myself to her. The woman I was and had always been: my accomplishments, new family, and happiness. We began texting nearly every day, then multiple times a day. We were both scared to speak with one another. We knew it was going to be emotional. And it was. After texting for a few weeks, we finally talked. We both cried at the sound of each other's voices. It felt like the first time you're reunited with a long-lost friend. It was for me—being reunited with a long-lost sister—a sister who wanted nothing to do with me for the majority of my life.

I soon discovered that spending time with her, even speaking with her on the phone, was a huge trigger. The toxic and oppressive relationship between my sister and me took a little over a year to reveal itself. I had to fully accept that it would be impossible to have a relationship with the woman who is my sister by DNA.

The fourteen months I reacquainted myself with Cindy were eye-opening. I wanted to believe that it had always been me as a child and adult who was to blame for the tear. It was easier for me to be the defect. To believe that I was the broken person in every relationship, that it was me that'd always been the issue: my bad behavior, my poor choices, my multiple marriages, my tumultuous relationship with our mother, quitting school, rebellious teenage years, speaking up, defending myself. It was easier for me to believe that all of these things, that had nothing to do with her, were reason enough for us not to have a relationship. It was easier to think that I had done something wrong to her so I could accept the way she pretended I didn't exist from the day we buried our mother to eleven years later when my life was happy, fulfilled, and toxin-free.

It had to be me.

Even her son, my grown nephew, an acclaimed scholar and tenured professor of Biology at the University of North Carolina–Chapel Hill, told her when he discovered we were trying to heal our broken relationship: "That's great, mom, just be careful and don't let her hurt you."

It seemed normal for her to be unsure of me as we sat on her oversized front porch, rekindling our sisterhood (I'd traveled twelve hundred miles, during a pandemic, to see her). It seemed normal to be the root of dysfunction of our family.

That was the comfortable space of self-deprecation I was used to.

Of course, my sister and her son would be cautious of me...I've always been the problem, the bad guy.

Once again, I shifted into my seven-year-old self, then my twelve-year-old self, sixteen and twenty-one, and the day of my mother's funeral when she was so cold and dismissive of me. That's where I went. Because that's where I allowed my sister and the rest of my family to keep me. So, I rolled with it, ensuring I didn't "hurt" her. I walked on eggshells, sensitive to her feelings so she and her son wouldn't be able to say, "She did it again. Jill will never change."

But I had changed—not for them, for *me*. They weren't my *why*; I was.

Throughout the year, I noticed behaviors that made me uncomfortable and kept dumping me back into the center of those toxic spaces, abandoning me. Eventually, I confronted her about a few things that were bothering me. It wasn't confrontational in my mind; well, it was in hers. We both got angry and, once again, aren't speaking to one another.

This is not to showcase petty conversations or who's in the right and the wrong, but how easy it was for us to slide back into a nonexistent relationship. That, along with the pattern of behavior I recognized, told me more than any conversation we could have had. I learned that I am okay without this person in my life.

The pain runs deep for both of us. And right now, we are not built for a relationship. We share blood, but we are not able to share in family. It is much too toxic on both sides.

I no longer sit inside this pain, and I choose not to soak in shame.

FOR MOST OF MY LIFE, I had a fantasy that once I achieved my personal best, my family, especially my sister, would love and accept me. That I would be enough. I dreamed about a reunion--a mending of broken pieces. And for a split second, with my sister, that fantasy was fulfilled. I dreamed of finally being included in family reunions, holiday gatherings, visits, and being welcomed with loving, open arms. I wrote the script. I dreamed of my family saying, "We always knew you could do it. We knew you had it in you. We love you. We accept you. You are one of us." A white-knuckle dream.

My mother used to tell me that everyone would accept me if I were a good person. I prescribed my own definition of that person grounded in what I learned as a child made a person worthy of love: a steady job, long marriage, college degrees, published author, etc. I was convinced my family would accept my accomplishments. But that never happened. In fact, things got worse the more I formed my own identity and asserted my voice.

As I grew into my identity, one of the shifts I made was understanding my beliefs from feminism to religion to politics. I grew up in a conservative household, and for most of my life, that was what I adopted as my own because that's what I was told was correct. It didn't take me long after I surrounded myself with like-minded people to fully understand why I felt the way I did and why I never fit in with the family that raised me.

Human emotions were supercharged during the 2020 presidential campaign and the four years preceding it. Family and friendships were ripped at the seams by hatred and divisiveness.

To those that know me, it is no secret that I vehemently disliked the dystopian Trump era and his Gilead-esque administration. There was nothing that I could do but idly stand by and accept what felt (and still feels) was one of the most disparaging times in American history. While I couldn't run for political office, I could use my voice for change. I was vocal about my likes and dislikes on social media. Although I certainly made anguished comments brought on by absolute exasperation, I tried to serve my opinions with a heavy dose of knowledge and truthful facts.

Most of my family doesn't follow me on social media, but there are a few here and there that don't interact with me yet do keep up with what I'm doing, mostly, I assume, because of their curiosity. They won't talk to me or acknowledge me in the flesh, but they will follow me on all my social media platforms. I did have a cousin, though, that I was very close to even though we supported different ideologies. We tolerated each other's opinions and steered clear conversations that would lead to confrontation.

George and I had never had a conflict. We grew up together; I was two years older than him. A few days after the votes for Joe Biden indicated a win, George posted something on his Facebook account that was downright inaccurate. I'd grown tired of the disinformation and chimed in by posting a response. I was harsh but factual. That was when his wife chimed in.

This person, my cousin's wife, I'd met approximately two times since her ten-year marriage with George. Suffice to say, she didn't know me. Her opinion of me was solely based on the toxic and incomplete stories the rest of my extended family told her over the years. She came after me like a bull charging its matador; however, her horns were a sheath of words and tangled inaccuracies that stabbed and sliced.

Her insults were loaded and the gaslighting plentiful. She closed out the public verbal lashing (behind the computer screen, I might add) with this comment, the full version being quite lengthy, so I'll just include a snippet, "We will not be listening to insults from a cluster f@#K like you. I'm just going to scream through Facebook what this entire family has wanted to scream for months.........STFU!!!!!!"

I have to admit, that got me. It took me out; it silenced me. I spiraled down a dangerous rabbit hole of dysfunction. I stepped away from my memoir for months. I couldn't write one more word about my past or my family. I allowed this insignificant person to trigger all the insecurities and self-doubts about myself. Shame was no longer living behind the walls; it was out front and center pulling me back into its suffocating grip. A few months and lots of work later, I acknowledged that I was a survivor of severe childhood trauma and suffered from PTSD—not a victim, a survivor. Victims quit. They curl up in a ball and give their abusers the power.

That was the breakthrough I'd been waiting for my entire life. I'd been hanging on to an idea that would never come to light: my family would never accept me. They don't know my story. They only know the subjective, twisted versions passed down through the years. None of them had enough concern to seek out the truth; they only sought out the stories they wanted to tell. This was my revelation. My awakening. My ticket to freedom. I finally let go of what could have been and chose to live in "what is."

I took my new power and lived. And I wasn't just living; I was thriving despite my family. Despite their stories and lies and inaccuracy and unknowing. I took their power away from my pain. I realized that by not engaging, I stripped them of their stronghold. I was giving the people in my family the power by hanging on, dreaming, and fantasizing about an alternate reality, one that I would never be a part of no matter what I did or didn't do. I re-gifted myself the power that I'd given away fifty years ago.

The tragedy in all of this is the confrontation between George's wife and I ended my relationship with my beloved cousin. It broke a forty-nine-year familial bond that, at one time, I considered unbreakable.

I will never again have the opportunity to make amends with George because COVID-19 took him first, less than a year after our fallout. I thought time was on our side. I thought the fires would calm one day, and we would repair what was broken.

We have time, I thought.

But he was gone before we ever had the chance at reparation.

IN ITS GAZILLIONTH week on the *New York Times* bestseller list, Glennon Doyle's *Untamed* guided me through the process of "Knowing." I uncovered my identity through contemplative stillness, through lived experiences, both positive and negative. When I allowed myself to sit through the pain instead of detaching and running, I came into my knowing.

"StopMovingStoptalkingStopSearchingStopPanickingStop-Flailing. If you just stop doing, you'll start knowing," Doyle says.

I stopped running, kicking, screaming, flailing. I sat in the stillness and listened to my soul. I'd never heard her speak. The voice was mine; I recognized her in an instant. She sounded whole. She'd been in there for far too long.

I'VE BEEN USING my voice to tell stories my entire life; although, it wasn't until about ten years ago that I discovered I had a gift and the courage to tell my own. For most of my life, I was a full-time, working musician singing and performing the stories of others. It was time I gave the little girl who was still crying to be heard a chance to speak.

I have forever had a penchant for words: finding and using them to connect myself with the world. Storytelling intersects language and life organically—it serves as a guide to humanity and the universe. Language holds the innate ability to jump off the page through a writer's deepest emotions. Nouns come to life symbolizing human connection—home, family, identity. Adjectives interconnect the five senses imbuing objects with meaning, inviting readers to discover their own vision of a told tale. A great storyteller embodies the inherent gift of setting every reader in the center of the world she creates. It's more than desire; it's a hunger void of satiety. That's what empowers me to write.

CHAPTER 14

We must learn to detach ourselves from the old stories in order to find the new ones.
~Jill Carlyle

Through all the pain, the unrelenting and overwhelming feeling of chaos, I've forged ahead with perseverance and purpose. I leaned into my goals and continued to meet them regularly, even if the journey took me the long way around. As I finished writing the final pages of this book, I was barely fifty-two years old. I have overcome hurdles I never thought I would find the strength to jump but knew I had the hops to do it.

As much as I love telling stories, writing my own has been the most difficult one I've told. I allow the inner critic, who keeps reminding me of other people's versions of me, to talk over me. It has literally stopped me in my tracks. For the last four years, that voice has tried its damnedest to scream louder than the most important one: mine. I had to detach myself from the old stories for me to bring them justice. I quit believing the ones I'd carried around in a tattered backpack that I refused to throw out. I stopped letting everyone else tell my story and did it myself. Once I did this, everything opened up.

The seven-year-old who learned her brother didn't want her around, the tween whose mother told her it would have been easier to accept a diagnosis of cancer than pregnancy, the thirteen-year-old whose father made her smoke an entire pack of cigarettes for experimenting with them, the pregnant sixteen-year-old who was forced to have an abortion, the woman with multiple marriages, the high school dropout: they are all me just as much as the fifty-something college graduate and professor is. Every age and every experience shaped the person I am. They built "me."

I spent years walking alone. At times the moments of solitude felt endless. But when I walked within the stillness of my truth, listening with intent to the sound of my personal silence, I heard the echoes of my soul taking me places I never dared to go. There's beauty in walking alone. Discovering the woman I am— the woman I am made to be. I opened my soul and allowed the silence and solitude to whisk me away into *me*.

What I discovered was a life-in-waiting. I am in control of my own destiny. There are no "keep-out" signs lurking from within —only the power and strength to walk through the doors waiting for me to enter.

I CLEARLY REMEMBER the day I walked into my first college course at Eastern Florida State College. I knew my future was full of possibilities, but what I didn't realize was that eight years later, I would return as a faculty member.

The day before I started my new job, my husband came into

my home office as I was putting the finishing touches on the upcoming week's lessons. He handed me a card and an oversized gift bag that was weighed down by its contents. I was surprised, not that Steve lacks in the gift-giving department, I just wasn't expecting anything—but that's always the best kind of gift, right?

I gently opened the card to read a handwritten message at the end: "Jill, I could not be more proud of you!! Congrats on the new career. Can't wait to see where it all leads. I love you! Love, Steve."

I stared at the card as the decade we've spent together played out in my mind. He was there for all of it. He loved and supported me through my full reset. He made sure I had everything I needed no matter what: computers, supplies, textbooks. He read every single one of my papers, learned about Jane Austen, lit theory, speculative fiction, and probably knows more about women writers than I do. Steve always made sure I was okay—even on the hard days. And we went through some hard ones. Here I was trying to make the wrong family (the insignificant people) accept me when I had the one person forever standing in front of me lifting me up.

I pulled the tissue paper off the top of the gift bag, which revealed the beautiful new rolling briefcase he bought me so it would be easy to navigate around campus. Steve was—*is*—the one who's always been there. My best friend, soulmate, and love of my life. He is my family.

Steve is Home. God heard my cry and answered my prayers all those years ago. It was all in His time.

As I ROLLED my new briefcase into the classroom to prepare for my first day as a professor, I stood alone in the middle of the room. It was a moment filled with emotion. The decisions I made to get there were filled with hope, self-love, and forgiveness. Tears that symbolize a milestone reached out of many to come from high school dropout to college professor.

This is how you fix shame, I thought to myself and prepared to teach my very first class of college students.

IN MEMORY OF

Mom
Dad
Larry
Kenny
My beloved cousin George
Oh, what a reunion it will be...
Love, ~J

What is severed in the flesh is made whole in the spirit.

ACKNOWLEDGMENTS

What started as a compilation of journal entries in my head turned into a 30,000-word master's thesis and shaped into 50,000 words of my heart. My story has been told after four years, a tear-stained keyboard, hundreds of pieces of paper, doubts, fears, exhaustion, and adversity. Thank you from the VERY depths of my soul for reading the black and white letters between this book's front and back cover. I appreciate you hearing me.

I spent years trying to figure out how to share these stories; the many iterations this book went through are the same for its author. With each one, I grew. I learned more about who I am and why I am—my truth. I learned to forgive myself and others along the way.

I learned that I am a survivor of childhood trauma, not a victim.

I took a ride with fear; however, I didn't let it drive. I made it to the finish line. But it's really only the beginning. And that's the beauty of standing inside the chaos and finally letting go.

This book was not a solo production. Although I was the only one who could "pen" my story, there were many people that held my hand through the process:

Lisa Marsh: Thank you for your developmental edit on *Finding Fifty.* You were the very first person to read my work in manuscript format and provide honest and applicable critiques. Your guidance helped me shape my story into a full-fledged book. Mostly, though, thank you for your friendship.

The Inner Circle Writing Community, specifically, the core group of you (us) that show up Monday-Friday for an hour. Finding and joining this group has been one of the biggest blessings of my writing career. Thank you for allowing me to bring my work to the table, graciously listening with open hearts, and always giving me supportive but constructive feedback. You all helped me find the *stamina* to keep going.

The University of Central Florida College of Arts and Humanities, to the fierce female educators that showed me how to be a *courageous* woman through the lens of other women's words and worlds.

Dr. Kathleen Oliver, thank you for introducing me to Aphra Behn and what it means to truly exude female agency.

Dr. Lisa Logan, thank you for introducing me to the world of women's literature.

Dr. Kathleen Hohenlietner, thank you for taking me on a journey with Jane Austen.

Professor Farrah Cato, I will never forget you. You helped me find my identity through strong female protagonists like Offred (*The Handmaid's Tale*), Essun (*The Fifth Season*), Lauren (*Parable of the Sower*), Sofi (*So Far from God*), Tan-Tan (*Midnight Robber*). I have taken parts of their world and inserted them into mine. Thank you for those gifts.

Danielle DeMiranda, My best friend of 30 plus years. I love you. You have been through everything, ALL OF IT with me. Yet you continue to love and show up for our friendship. *YOU are my Ride or Die.*

Rachel Taillefer, we started Accountability Saturdays in mid-August 2021 to support our writing—but it has become much more. I genuinely cherish you and your friendship. You are special to me for so many reasons. Your unwavering support every week when we've gathered on our Saturday afternoon Zoom calls—you in NYC and me in Florida—helped guide me through not only finishing my memoir but taught me things about myself I'd been too afraid to recognize on my own. Our conversations impacted and changed me (for the better!) I am so grateful to have you in my life!

Dr. Madeline Smith, we were meant to meet. Thank you for your friendship, mentorship, and sisterhood. I know it will span a lifetime.

Yildirim Danisman, my photographer. Thank you for your vision and beautiful artwork.

Onur Aksoy, thank you for the beautiful cover design.

Professor Amy Butcher, thank you for seeing me, guiding me, mentoring me, hearing me, and helping me take my story to the page.

Shuna Morelli, thank you for gifting this work with your gracious words. I am humbled. I cherish your insight but am especially grateful for your friendship.

And finally, my husband, **Steve Carlyle**. Thank you for showing me unconditional love and believing in this project from its inception. You are my person. I love you.

ABOUT THE AUTHOR

Jill Carlyle is an emerging author of both fiction and nonfiction work. She is a graduate of the University of Central Florida and holds a Bachelor of Arts in English Literature and a double master's degree in English and Creative Nonfiction from Southern New Hampshire University. She is pursuing an additional Master of Fine Arts (MFA) in Creative Fiction. Jill is an adjunct professor of English Composition and Literature at Eastern Florida State College in Cocoa, Florida.

For more information visit:
www.jillcarlylewrites.com

facebook.com/JillWritesaBook
twitter.com/jcarlylewrites
instagram.com/jillcarlylewrites

Made in the USA
Middletown, DE
16 February 2022

61295404R00111